BREAKAWAY

Also by Alex Morgan

The Kicks

Saving the Team

Sabotage Season

Win or Lose

Hat Trick

by ALEX MORGAN
with Sarah Durand

SIMON & SCHUSTER BFYR

NEW YORK   LONDON   TORONTO   SYDNEY   NEW DELHI

An imprint of Simon & Schuster Children's Publishing Division
1230 Avenue of the Americas, New York, New York 10020
SIMON & SCHUSTER BFYR is a trademark of Simon & Schuster, Inc.
For information about special discounts for bulk purchases, please contact
Simon & Schuster Special Sales at 1-866-506-1949
or business@simonandschuster.com.
The Simon & Schuster Speakers Bureau can bring authors to your live event. For
more information or to book an event, contact the Simon & Schuster Speakers
Bureau at 1-866-248-3049 or visit our website at www.simonspeakers.com.
Jacket design by Krista Vossen
Interior design by Hilary Zarycky
The text for this book is set in Berling.
Manufactured in the United States of America
2 4 6 8 10 9 7 5 3 1
Library of Congress Cataloging-in-Publication Data
Morgan, Alex (Alexandra Patricia), 1989–
Breakaway / Alex Morgan. — First edition hardcover.
pages cm
ISBN 978-1-4814-5107-9 (Hardcover) — ISBN 978-1-4814-5109-3 (Ebook)
1. Morgan, Alex (Alexandra Patricia), 1989– 2. Women soccer players—United
States—Biography—Juvenile literature. I. Title.
GV942.7.M673A3 2015
796.334092—dc23
[B]
2015004127

FIRST
EDITION

To my parents, Pam and Mike;
my mother-in-law, Gloria;
and my husband, Servando,
for their advice and guidance

BREAKAWAY

Preface

Something wasn't right. Actually, something was really wrong. The pain in my right knee was sharp, and it wouldn't stop.

A minute ago I'd been a normal seventeen-year old, with a position on a national soccer team and an athletic scholarship to one of the best colleges in the country, and now I was lying on the field clutching my knee as if that would make the pain go away.

"Help! Something's not right. I'm hurt," I whimpered to the boy who was kneeling next to me. "I think I need some help."

Maybe I should have been angry at him, but I was too worried about my knee. I knew he hadn't meant to injure me. I'd been chasing him down, and when I'd reached him, I'd tried to block his kick. But he'd faked and cut the ball to avoid me. I'd tried to cut him in return, but my body had gone right and my knee had gone left. I'd felt immediate pain, and as emotions flooded over me, I'd realized within a millisecond that

I couldn't walk. Something was very, very wrong.

I tried to focus on something, anything, to take my mind away from the pain. *Think positive thoughts, Alex. It's a beautiful day in Southern California. You've just received a soccer scholarship to Cal, and you're playing on a national team. Everything's coming together, and you're going to be okay.*

My team had been scrimmaging with the men's junior national soccer team when I fell. It was fun, not too serious, but a good way for me to develop as a player and challenge myself. I'd always liked training with boys. Maybe it was because I have two sisters, so being around boys was sort of exciting and different.

My dad had always been my biggest supporter, and in fact, he was at practice that day watching me. While I couldn't see him, I assumed he was rushing toward the field to find out what was going on. Despite my pain, I smiled at the thought of him. He always encouraged me, and some of my fondest memories were of practicing with him.

"Corners, corners, shoot for the corners!" he would say. "Head down, follow the ball into the net."

Oh, Dad, I thought. Did he really think I didn't know the basics of soccer when I was sixteen years old? I owed so much to him. He'd gone to all my games, and we practiced together at least twice a week. Sometimes four or five times. We would go across the street to the middle school. If that field was occupied, we would go to Pantera Park. If people were on that field, we'd go to Peterson Park. He never gave up.

I couldn't let him down. He wouldn't get mad if I moved on to something else—he never pressured me about soccer, or anything, really—but I knew I was poised for something great, and I wanted him and Mom to be proud of me. I wanted to play for Cal; I wanted to feel an Olympic gold medal around my neck; and I wanted to win the World Cup. I had goals, and I was determined to meet them.

But first I had to stand up, get off the field, and figure out what was wrong with my knee.

Note to the Reader

I have always set goals for myself. Even when I was little, I had hopes—big and small—about everything. They mostly centered on soccer, but to me soccer is life. It's not just a game; it's a way of thinking, dreaming, and being. But you don't have to be a soccer player to have wishes and hopes. You can have objectives no matter what you do. And if there's anything I've learned, it's that you don't have to meet your goals on your first try, or even your tenth. Setting targets and working toward them is what counts. And it's so important never to forget that.

When I was lying on that soccer field, so many thoughts were running through my seventeen-year-old head, but most of them centered on the goals I'd set for myself. I'll talk more about that awful afternoon and what happened in the days and weeks after it, but thinking back on that day, I wish I'd realized that a setback doesn't mean you won't reach your goals someday. I've had so many big bumps in the road in my life, but they've all taught me something. They've shown me how to accept challenges, work hard to overcome them, and in the end, forge a path toward my true purpose.

I hope this book helps you discover the many ways that you can go after your dreams. I'm so young that my life is really just beginning, and yours probably is too. But being on the soccer field has taught me some really important lessons, specifically about setting goals and embracing your passions. I've learned that life can be wonderful if you have the right attitude, work hard, and dream big, and my wish is that reading this will help you set the objectives that will make each day richer and fuller than the last.

—Alex

I was doing things my own way even before I was born. After having two girls, my parents wanted a boy. Not that having a third girl is a bad thing; they just wanted something different. But I had my own set of plans, and when I was born on July 2, 1989, there I was: a little baby girl.

With each child my parents had had an agreement. If they had a boy, my dad would choose the name, and if they had a girl, my mom would have the honor. My mom settled on the name Alexandra for me. I can only guess that's because my dad had chosen the "boy name" Alexander, and my mom decided to allow him just the smallest bit of influence.

What's so funny is that even though my dad doted on his girls, he had a real vision of how he would have raised his son, if he'd had one. He once said that since I was the third girl, "he was going to make a boy out of me somehow." He was joking, of course—he *loves* having three girls and wouldn't trade us for anything—but

I think he had certain hopes as a father. My dad grew up playing baseball, and he dreamed of a son playing it, living out what *he'd* loved most as a little boy.

I'm getting ahead of myself, though. Way before my dad helped introduce me to athletics, I was just a little kid growing up in Diamond Bar, California, about twenty-five miles east of Los Angeles. Diamond Bar is a nice suburban community—quiet, sunny, and generally happy. I liked it there. Mostly everyone knew one another, and I was able to walk to elementary and middle school.

But there wasn't very much going on in Diamond Bar. It was a *huge* deal when we got a Target, and we didn't even have a chain restaurant until I was fifteen or so. It's the kind of place that you're happy to grow up in but also happy to get out of once you come of age. I think so much of my youth revolved around sports precisely because not much else happened around me.

My parents basically grew up together. My dad was best friends with my mom's older brother, and he's as close with my mom's siblings as she is. In fact, he probably sees them even more than she does! My parents starting dating on and off when my mom was eighteen or so, and they got married and had my eldest sister when she was twenty-three and he was thirty-four.

My dad owned and ran a small construction company,

and my mom worked with him until she decided to get her master's degree when I was about six. My two older sisters, Jenny and Jeri, were my best friends. Jenny is six years older than me, and Jeri is four years older. I was very close to Jeri, experiencing intense ups and downs like you do with your friends, and Jenny was a little more of a mother figure to me, especially when my mom went back to school at night. She happily dove into a care-taking role and began cooking for the family and orga-nizing things for us while our mom was at class.

I was always in their shadow. When you're the third kid, it's just like that. You're considered "the baby." And my mom always got us confused! When she'd call me for something, she'd say, "Jenny! Jeri! I mean Alex!" She definitely valued us as individuals, but three girls can be a whirlwind!

My parents were stricter with me than they were with my sisters. Even though I was kind of sweet and shy and not at all a troublemaker, they held me to a higher standard. Maybe they knew my potential, or maybe they wanted to do everything right for their last child.

I remember we used to play so many games. Family games on Wednesday nights were always a big deal, espe-cially with my dad. We'd play gin rummy or Monopoly or other board games, and they were really competitive. That's where I got my fighting spirit; competition was a positive thing in our house, not a negative one. There were always winners and losers, though—nobody would be handed a win out of pity. My mom was actually the only one who wouldn't laugh in your face when she won. If it was just me and her, the outcome of the game really didn't matter. But not my dad! He would literally do a dance around the house after he won. It was *extremely* annoying.

Like I said, competition was all in good fun, but I'm not sure how fun Jeri thought it was when I first beat her in a footrace. I'd always been one step behind her in everything, but when I was nine I realized I was pretty fast and I might have a chance at doing something better than her. I'd stopped thinking my name was "Jeri's little sister" instead of Alex, and I was going to assert myself!

"I'm going to beat you! You've got no chance. I'm going to win," Jeri yelled at me as we were about to race against each other at the school across from our house.

"Just you watch me," I said as I took off running.

Jeri couldn't even keep up—I crossed the finish line way before her. I'm sure she'd deny it to this day, but I remember it clearly. I totally killed her.

My dad really wanted us to be athletic, and we all played different sports when we were little. I played soccer, softball, basketball, volleyball, and even participated in local track meets, which I loved.

I was probably three when I really learned how to catch a ball, and that was when Dad decided I was destined for softball. My sisters had been playing in a softball league for years, so I'd seen lots of their games. I remember holding on to the fence outside one of their games, poking my nose through as I cheered them on. Dad signed me up for a team as soon as I was old enough, and from then on I played softball more often and more intensely than any other sport. The first team I played on was a T-ball team called the A's, and it was, of course, coached by my dad.

Jenny and Jeri were really good at school, but I took to athletics a little more than them, so I think that's when my dad started pushing me harder than them. It wasn't in a bad way—he just nudged me to do something I seemed naturally inclined toward and that I liked.

We would go to Anaheim Angels baseball games all the time. My dad had season tickets for a few years, and every time we went, he made sure that I brought my glove just in case I caught a foul ball. It was always so fun going to games, but now that I'm so into soccer, I look back and think, *Wow, baseball is boring. Why did I enjoy it so much?* Maybe it was just because I liked making my dad proud.

One day when I was about nine, though, I decided I'd

had enough. I'd been playing soccer since I was five, and I'd realized that it was the sport for me.

I turned to my dad and said, "You know what? I don't like softball."

"What?" I could see the shocked look on my dad's face. I was so good! How was it possible that I didn't like it?

"I like soccer. I like to run."

Dad's face visibly softened. You see, he just wanted me to be happy and to chase my dreams. His goal—for me to love softball as much as he loved baseball—wasn't the most important thing. He just wanted me to follow my passion, whatever it was. And it was clear that my passion was soccer.

Pushing Moves You Forward

There's probably someone really important in your life who pushes you toward a goal—it could be your teacher, your mom, your grandfather, or someone else entirely— and you might disagree with them sometimes. I disagreed with my dad all the time! But I think you still need to value their place in your life. If you listen to them and let them in, they will probably nudge you just a little harder to find your passion. I'll always thank my dad for doing that for me.

CHAPTER 2

You probably have a soccer league in your town. Most places do, as soccer is, believe it or not, the third most played sport in America right now, behind basketball and baseball. Thirty percent of households in the United States have at least one member who plays the game. People began to pay attention to professional soccer in 1994, when the United States hosted the men's World Cup, but for girls, 1999 will always be the year that women's soccer exploded. That's when the United States won the women's World Cup. But more on that later. . . .

In Diamond Bar, soccer was a really big deal for kids. Every kid I knew played recreationally, and the AYSO—the American Youth Soccer Organization—had a few great leagues right around us. I loved soccer right away, and unlike with my sisters, who eventually gave up the sport, that never changed. We'd run around so much as kids that taking off down the field came naturally for me. I was *really* fast, and I loved to go for the ball. I was always kind of a tomboy, too. I didn't dress like a boy, but I loved playing with the guys and beating them. For example, when we'd run for charity at my elementary school, I took so much joy in getting a better time than all the boys. That's part of the reason I gravitated to soccer—I could play with boys just as easily as I could play with girls.

I started dreaming big about soccer when I was around eight. I just loved it. I counted the minutes till I was on the field, and I had a blast with my friends during practices and games. Plus, getting better and better at soccer gave me a goal to reach for. I wrote a letter to my mom when I was eight, and I'm so glad she kept it because it really says a lot about where my head was then.

My dad didn't know a thing about the sport, though, and he didn't really want anything to do with it in the beginning. He just didn't understand why people liked it. Of course he supported me and my sisters, but he wasn't involved in the beginning like he was with softball.

But he started to get serious when he began paying attention and better understanding the game. At age nine, I started practicing with him—not just doing drills and making shots but also running. He would have me practice with ankle weights for a few laps; then I would take off the weights and run like I was flying. I'm not sure if it helped at all with my speed, but it definitely helped with my endurance.

My dad also wanted so badly to nurture my natural ability that he took coaching lessons and bought one of those pop-up goals so that we could play in our yard. Pretty soon he wasn't just coaching me on my own; he was heading up my AYSO teams. On the years he didn't coach, he and my mom didn't miss a single one of my games. And they even hired a speed coach for me when I was ten!

As my dad learned more about soccer, he got more interested in technique and he began to focus on my ability to finish. When we'd play in the yard, he'd stress again and again that making a shot is one thing but *finishing* is another. Finishing is actually getting the ball to go where you want in the goal, most often low and in the corners.

"Dad, I'm tired. I think we should just do finishing tomorrow," I remember saying.

"But, Al, you gotta work hard every day if you want to be the best. Well, you are the best, but you can be better. Come on. We'll get ice cream from 7-Eleven after."

And that would work, every time.

Now that I think about it, finishing in soccer is a lot like following through with a goal in life. It's one thing to try to make a goal, but it's another to pursue a precise path toward that dream. Sometimes the path may not be clear, but when it is, you should go for it. I have no idea if my dad had made that connection at the time, but the lessons he taught me about finishing stick with me to this day.

During the summer of 1999, when I was ten years old, things *really* changed for me. That was the golden summer, when Mia Hamm, Julie Foudy, Kristine Lilly, Brandi Chastain, and the rest of the national soccer team exploded onto the international scene and captured the World Cup title. The team's overtime win in the final against China ended weeks of some of the most dramatic play the world had ever seen. I'd watched so many games on TV, but that final was on a whole different level.

I especially loved Kristine Lilly—she was the kind of

forward I wanted to be. She was fast and hardworking, and she could change a game instantly—her quiet energy was infectious. She wore #13, and I play in that number in her honor. I met her briefly at a youth national team camp when I was sixteen. She met with us in the locker room at the StubHub Center just to say hi and give a few words of inspiration. Honestly, I couldn't even tell you what she said. But I remember the way she carried herself, so confident and comfortable in her own skin. She was so content with her life and her accomplishments, but she still wanted to meet me. I couldn't believe it. *That's* how I want to be with my fans.

But back to the 1999 World Cup. The final was being held in Pasadena at the Rose Bowl, which was *so close* to Diamond Bar. I didn't get to go, so I was glued to the TV screen when the final began. There were ninety thousand people at the Rose Bowl—still the highest attendance any women's sporting event has ever seen—and the excitement was so intense that I could practically feel it thirty miles away.

I watched every minute of that game, and when it went into a penalty shoot-out after remaining scoreless during all of regulation and two periods of extra time, I was breathless. When Brandi Chastain netted the final penalty kick, then fell to her knees and tore off her shirt in celebration, I screamed with joy.

That is going to be me someday, I decided. *When I grow up, I am going to play in the World Cup final. And I am going to win.*

Find a Mentor

Even if someone in your life doesn't help you out the way my parents did for me—I realize I was *really* lucky—you can still seek out guidance from someone. I was shy, so I know how hard it is to speak up, but there are teachers and coaches out there who really want to help. But you have to ask them. Having a mentor or a role model, even if it's just for a few weeks, will teach you something, and that person may end up being in your life for years! So don't be afraid to seek out help, wherever it may be.

CHAPTER 3

I kept playing with AYSO a few more years after the "golden summer," but when I was about thirteen, it was clear that I was getting so good that I needed to step up my training. I was already taking things *pretty* seriously—I was practicing soccer every day, I'd made it clear that it was my favorite sport, and in my mind, it was what I was destined to do for the rest of my life. But I hadn't *truly* put that plan in motion.

There's a difference between dreaming and doing, and I think you have to really act on something to live out your dreams. You can't just hope to be a star. You need to think ahead and work through the necessary steps to make things happen. I'm not saying that you have to have a ten-point action plan and beat every single deadline, but you do need to work and work and never hesitate to take that next step. If you want to be an artist, don't just dream and dabble in your school's art class. Seek out classes at your local museum. If you want to be a scientist, don't just join your school's Science

Bowl. Call up a researcher at the local university and ask to do an informational interview with them. Or if you're nowhere near a college, e-mail them! They'll probably be thrilled to hear from you.

That next step for me was club soccer. Club is more serious than AYSO—you actually have to try out for it. And you don't just play teams in your town—you travel all over the state and sometimes around the country if you get into a national tournament. Colleges recruit out of club teams (in addition to high school teams), so anytime you're playing, there may be someone up in the stands watching you, trying to figure out if you should get a scholarship or not. It's pretty serious, but I was ready.

The only thing standing in my way was my age. Most kids start in club soccer when they're eight or nine, and I was thirteen! Four years is a lifetime in soccer, so I really had to prove myself.

Unfortunately, that didn't happen right away. My first tryout for club wasn't successful—I didn't get on the team. Instead, I was put in as a "practice player." And I was shocked.

I talk about that experience a lot when I speak with girls about motivation. That year of club was the first time I actually "wasn't good enough." I had been one of the best—if not *the* best—on every team I had played on, and that season, reality slapped me in the face. I knew I needed to develop as a player. I had raw talent, but I hadn't learned many soccer smarts in AYSO. Plus, the girls on the club team were cold to me. And, sure, sometimes thirteen-year-olds can be catty. But more than that, I just felt out of place. I missed my old friends so much. They were all still playing with AYSO teams, having fun and not taking things as seriously as I felt I had to. Maybe that was part of the reason I'd waited so long to try out for club—not just because I wanted to keep playing with my friends, but because I was worried about what a heavy commitment a club team would be.

Looking back, it was good I'd waited a bit to join a club team. I think I needed to be a little more mature to handle the stress. People, especially young athletes, take things so seriously now. There's so much pressure to get scholarships, and it starts younger and younger every year. Yet I know people who started on a club team when they were eight or nine and burned out or started to hate the sport. I'm glad that didn't happen to me.

I'm not a quitter, though, so as uncomfortable as I felt on that club team, I kept going to practice. I vowed, *I'm going to prove the coach and my teammates wrong. I'm going to go to practice every day and get better.*

Practice I did, but the coach still didn't put me in. And after about three months I decided I'd had enough. I told my coach that I was moving on to a different club, where I could actually play. Those three months had felt like a year to me. But what made that period of time bearable was that everyone up until that point in my life had believed in me. My family, my former teammates, and all my previous coaches had always encouraged me, and their influence drove me to try to prove that first club coach wrong.

My new club team was closer to home—this one only a five-minute drive away, where we played at the local park. In this case, though, the team wasn't competitive enough. I quickly learned that I *should* be on a better team, pushing myself and competing with players as committed as I wanted to be.

When I was fourteen, I got that chance. I tried out for a team called Cypress Elite, and I made the cut. The team was based in Orange County, south of Los Angeles, so I was going to have to travel a little bit to practices. But if I was going to have a career in soccer, a top-notch team was the next step, so I was prepared to do whatever I had to do. I was thrilled when I got onto Cypress, but I didn't know then what a huge influence it was going to be on my life.

Attitude Is Everything

As you chase your goals, it's hard to change the world or the people around you, but you can definitely change yourself. My first experience on a club team was terrible, and I was miserable a lot of the time. I had to stay positive and remember that I wasn't the disappointment my coach and teammates thought I was. If you go through a tough time like this, know that your attitude can make all the difference. Think positive and focus on the fact that you're working toward your dreams, and your dreams are exciting! It may be hard, but don't let the pressures around you get you down. You hold the key to your own happiness.

CHAPTER 4

My first steps onto the field in Cypress, California, where my team was located, were rocky, but I didn't know it at the time. I just loved to play, and I loved to run, and I was eager to get going. My coach, Dave Sabet, told us to sprint onto the field in our first practice, and I simply took off.

"She just blew by all my club players," Dave later said. "But the thing about her was, she didn't have any sort of idea. No skill. She just had phenomenal speed."

So apparently all that training with AYSO and with Dad hadn't taught me real technique! Sure, I'd practiced finishing and done some drills, but it wasn't enough to get to where I wanted to go. I hadn't realized the degree to which soccer is an art, something that requires you to continually work on craft and precision. I guess that's why I was now playing in the big leagues—not to learn how to play harder, but to play *better*.

It's important to focus on the details in whatever you do, and that's what club soccer began to teach me. It taught me to stop, study the specifics, and practice them till they're perfect. This isn't limited to soccer, of course. You might be a budding chef, but learning how to master the basic skills, like holding a knife, will make all the difference in how you progress. Having good teachers will help you with that, and that's what my Cypress coaches did for me. For four years, Dave and his assistant coaches, Sal and Eduardo, were my biggest influences on the field.

Dave, Sal, and Eduardo worked as a three-man team. They were tireless. They would come early and train with me, or I would stay late and do extra training and shooting with them.

Dave had been coaching for years, so he had a wealth of experience. He did most of my training—before, during, and after practice—and always focused on the little things. And Eduardo was wonderful in terms of emotional support. He was a huge fan of the team and always pushed us to do well.

Sal helped me analyze my game, and in fact, he still does! He's a real jokester, and my teammates and I always felt comfortable talking to him off the field about problems we were having. I still speak with him pretty regularly and have gone back to Cypress to help out with the Friday clinics he and Eduardo run.

Apparently I was learning pretty quickly, because within six months of joining Cypress I got a call to go to the Cal South ODP (Olympic Development Program). ODP is a program that identifies players who show promise for the national scene and helps prepare them to play at that level. Joining ODP didn't mean that I had to leave Cypress, though. It was just one additional thing for me to focus on.

ODP is an amazing program that has trained some of the best athletes in the game: Landon Donovan, my national teammates Shannon Boxx, Rachel Buehler, and Amy Rodriguez, and legends Joy Fawcett and Julie Foudy. Being part of a system that had coached these stars was more than an honor. It made me realize I was a serious competitor.

Things got even *more* serious when I was recruited for the under-17 national team. The youth national coaches had found me through ODP, and I played with the team for a year, from ages sixteen to seventeen. Because the first U-17 World Cup was held in 2008, I never got to play in it, but going to tournaments with the team gave me my first real exposure to international players. I'd always played only against Americans, but with U-17 I was competing against other women from around the globe.

Between Cypress, ODP, and the U-17 national team, I was traveling almost every weekend, often without my parents. I learned so much about balance—I had to juggle schoolwork, my high school soccer team, my family, and my social life. In 2006, my sister Jenny got married, and I skipped the rehearsal dinner because I was participating in a U-17 training camp! Luckily, the camp wasn't too far from the wedding venue, so I didn't miss the actual ceremony, but I did drive back to camp that night because I had a game the next day.

If you're passionate about something, you'll have to make sacrifices like this. There's no time to sit around doing nothing, and you're not going to be able to do everything or be everywhere. If you want to pursue your dreams, you have to concentrate on them every day. But that's where dedication comes in. If you love something as much as I love soccer, it's much easier to be dedicated and to make the balancing act worthwhile.

If you're serious about sports, I think you also have to realize that the chances of becoming a professional athlete who can make a living from your sport *for the rest of your life* are small. That's why you have to stay focused on school. I'm not saying you have to put your dreams aside—far from it. But doing your best in school should be a priority too. Again, it's all about balance. I was a scholar-athlete all four years of high school, and it's one of my proudest accomplishments. Good grades don't just ensure you'll get into a good college; doing well in school opens the door to a multitude of careers that you can turn to after your athletic career ends. You might eventually want to be a lawyer, start your own company, or become a writer. You may not yet know what you want to do after high school or college. But it's important to remember there's life after sports, and focusing on school now will prepare you for whatever is to come.

In my time with Cypress we won some championships—the Cal South Cup for the under-16 group in particular—and as I watched my game get better and better, I realized my goal of playing professionally was getting closer. But I discovered it was something I couldn't do alone. One of the major things I learned while playing for Cypress was the importance of teamwork. When I'd practiced with my dad, it was just me and him—no one else to pass to, no one else to wait for a pass from. It was just shoot and score. While that's important, it's usually not what happens on the soccer field. Most of the time you depend on teammates to assist you with a goal.

During all those years I played on recreational teams, I don't think I valued the importance of team play as much as I should have. My teammates were my friends, of course, but they weren't what I liked best about the game. Winning was what I loved (that, and running). But now that I was learning lots of new techniques and plays, I realized that what you most need to win at the highest level are your teammates.

In 2004 I went to Mia Hamm, Julie Foudy, and Joy Fawcett's retirement game at the Home Depot Center in Carson, California, which was a little less than an hour from Diamond Bar. While I was watching them, I remember thinking, *That's going to be me someday. I'm going to be like these women.* I decided I was *really* ready to work to achieve success at the highest levels. Sitting there in the stands that day, I also thought about how beautifully they'd played not just in 1999, but on every team they'd been on. None of these women achieved success on their own—they always had a team they trusted and relied on for support. Soccer isn't about personal glory. It truly is a team effort.

Find a Partner

As I said, realizing the importance of a team was a huge revelation to me when I started playing club soccer. You may be doing something on the individual level—working toward becoming valedictorian of your class or the lead clarinet in your school orchestra—but finding a partner to practice with might really motivate you. Find a study buddy or someone to jam with. That person may teach you important lessons or be a great sounding board for your ideas, frustrations, and accomplishments.

CHAPTER 5

During my junior year I began to look at colleges. College might still be a few years away for you, or it might be around the corner. If it's something you've started thinking about, know that deciding on a college may not be easy. Just focus on what you want out of the college years. What are your priorities? I had narrowed my options down to what was important to me—a California school with good academics *in addition to* a great soccer program. I probably won't make a living from soccer forever, so making sure I had a strong academic background was vital for me.

Because I'd attracted national attention on the U-17 squad, college recruiters came to me. Recruiters aren't allowed to call students before August of their junior year, but they can send them letters before that. For me, the letters began arriving when I was a sophomore, and the calls came at the beginning of my junior year. But some promising young athletes receive letters as early as middle school!

Recruiters have to balance whom to give scholar-ships to, so it's in their best interest to start the process as soon as possible. I wanted to be sure I found the right place for me, so my dad and I took it upon ourselves to look into certain colleges before I was in contact with the coaches, when the pressure would really set in. I even visited a few before I was recruited. Finding the best fit in a university could be tough, and I wanted to be sure I made the right decision at the end of it all. One thing made my decision easier, though: I knew I wanted to stay in California, so I turned away a lot of schools.

If you're a high school athlete, you may not be recruited, but that doesn't mean you can't play at the college level. You can visit the NCAA's website to get more information, or you can talk to your high school coach or college counselor for more information. You can also call a college's athletic department, and they can give you information. And there are plenty of people who've been walk-on athletes in college, which means they tried out for their varsity squads. Have you heard of Santana Moss, the Pro Bowl NFL star who plays for the Redskins? He was a walk-on for the Miami Hurricanes. Scottie Pippen, Jordy Nelson, and Brett Gardner were also college walk-ons, and they're legends!

I went to Pepperdine, USC, UC Berkeley (called Cal for short), the University of San Diego, Santa Clara, and Stanford on recruitment visits. What's funny is that when I toured USC I shared a dorm room with Amy Rodriguez, who was a freshman at the time and is now my teammate on the national team! But I didn't know her at all back then.

When you do end up visiting colleges or talking to your friends and family about them, try to remember what's important to you. Other people's opinions might influence you, but as much as possible, stick to your values. If you're recruited, you might feel a lot of outside pressure, but try to stay focused on what you really need. What's right for one person may not be right for you. In fact, if you visit a college with a friend or family member, you may see the exact same things but experience them differently. For example, here's what happened to me and my friend Allison when we went to Stanford and Cal.

When we toured Stanford, we walked the campus, met the soccer coach, watched a game, and then spent the night. I remember thinking, *I don't think this is for me.* But Allison kept saying, "Oh my gosh. This place is amazing. I love it. It's gorgeous. Isn't it great?"

And I was sitting there thinking, *Not really.*

Then we went to Cal the next day, and I started cooing. "This place is so great! It's liberal, and there are people selling things on the street! It's so free-spirited and so fun and different from where I grew up!"

And Allison replied, "I can't wait to go home. This is not what I want."

So she ended up going to Stanford, and I ended up going to Cal.

If you're going to play on an NCAA team, chances are you'll sign what's called a letter of intent. This seals your commitment to the college team. I signed a letter of intent for Cal my junior year, but I still had to formally apply my senior year. I was so excited when I was admitted. Like I said, I chose it because I was ready for a change and because both the academic and soccer programs were strong.

My acceptance to Cal reinforced something I'd suspected all along, too, and something I still feel to this day. If you're a serious athlete and really want a college athletic scholarship, don't break your back and stress yourself out early on, like when you're thirteen. Recruiters are looking seriously at young athletes early on—starting in middle school—but that doesn't mean you have to be 100 percent perfect that young. A lot changes between ages thirteen and eighteen. I was certainly not at my best when I started club. As you might remember, I had no skill, just speed. I wasn't noticed by recruiters until I was at least sixteen. This holds true for more than athletics. If you're a debater, for example, don't stress out if you're not the best on the debate team when you're fourteen.

Just believe in yourself and work hard. Recruiters or college teams will find you if you're the kind of person they're looking for. And you can also approach a school or try out when you arrive on campus.

By the time I was considering colleges, recruiters had found me. In my mind, I was at the prime of my young life. I was ready for college, loving my senior year, and excited about my future. I thought I'd checked off all the boxes I needed to check off that year, and I felt confident about what lay ahead for me.

Little did I know it would all change in an instant.

Set Your Own Timeline

As I said above, don't kick yourself too hard if you're not perfect or if you haven't met your goal by a random date set by other people. I was far from perfect at thirteen, fourteen, or fifteen, and in fact, I'm still not perfect! Pursuing your dreams is an ongoing process, and it's something you need to do for yourself—not to meet another person's timeline. Just set a goal for yourself to be as good as you can be, and make your deadlines your own. No one else should tell you how and when to meet your goals.

CHAPTER 6

I had been having such a good time practicing against the men's junior national team that afternoon during the winter of my senior year. I was joined by the rest of the women's U-17 national team, and our scrimmage was going well. I was truly happy—so much in my life had come together, and the world was at my fingertips.

And then I fell down and felt a sharp pain tear through my right knee.

When I finally rose to my feet, I hobbled over to the sidelines with my arms wrapped around two other players.

"Thanks, guys," I said, and I meant it. By then I'd learned that other players feel a deep sense of concern when you're injured. Even if they're not on your team, they don't want to see you out of the game. Maybe it's because they fear being there themselves, or because they really care about your well-being, or because a hurt player really dampens the mood on the field. Regardless, they usually rush to your aid.

My dad was there at practice, as always. When I got to my feet and away from the field, he helped me into the car, and even though I knew he felt as helpless as I did, he was trying to console me the whole time. My mom met us at the hospital. We sat down with an orthopedic surgeon, who ordered an MRI, and as I lay in the room with my parents awaiting the results, I expressed my biggest fears.

"Mom, Dad, I know how these things go. If this is bad, I may be out of the game forever. Soccer is my life. I don't want that."

My mom was so kind. "Alex, no matter what, soccer is going to be in your life. This is not going to end your dreams. I know you, and I know how hard you're going to fight to get back on the field. You've always won— always. You're going to beat this knee injury just like you've beaten everything else." Mom smiled at me as she held my hand, squeezing it tightly.

As much as I wanted to believe her comforting words, I couldn't stop the barrage of negative thoughts that were going through my head. If I couldn't play soccer, I'd lose my scholarship to Cal. I wouldn't be able to finish my final season with my high school team. And worst of all, I'd be without a direction. For the longest time, soccer had been my main focus in life. It had taught me about teamwork, dedication, passion, hard work, and setting goals. Where else was I going to find something I loved as much?

You might have had an experience that sent you into the depths of despair. Maybe it was a death in the family, an injury, or even something simple like a bad grade. And while you're going through it, it might feel like the end of the world. But trust me, it's not. You're still alive and breathing, and you still have years and years ahead of you to make something wonderful out of your life. A setback is a challenge, but it's not the end of your dreams. I didn't realize it at that moment, but my injury would teach me that.

The doctor came back into the room. "Alex, I have the results."

I took a deep breath.

"It's a torn ACL. It's probably going to require surgery and then physical therapy, but you'll be back on the field in less than six months."

I felt myself exhale. I'd known lots of players who had torn ACLs, and most of them had come back and played brilliantly. If they could do it, I could too.

You might have heard of the ACL, but if you haven't, I'll explain it. ACL stands for "anterior cruciate ligament," and it's one of the four major ligaments that hold your knee together. When you bend your knee, your ACL stretches to allow that motion. Essentially, it's what holds the bones of your knee together and stabilizes it when you bend or pivot. That's why it often tears in sports—because you're bending, turning, moving side to side, and in general, putting a lot of strain on your knees.

During surgery, an orthopedic surgeon usually takes tissue from another part of your body and puts it into your knee, essentially patching up the tear. It's an incredibly common type of surgery, and in fact, ACL injuries are one of the most frequent problems sports medicine doctors see. After surgery, a person may need as long as six months for recovery, during which time they go through physical therapy to strengthen the knee.

I wasn't looking forward to being out for so long, but I was relieved that the injury wasn't worse.

When I got home that day, I mentally prepared myself for what was to come. I was going to have to go to rehab to alleviate the swelling in my knee. Then I was going to have surgery. After that, I knew I was going to have to give myself the space and time to recover. I couldn't push myself to the limit—that would only make the injury worse. And I knew if I got impatient I'd only get more frustrated. I was frustrated enough already. I couldn't imagine what I'd be like if it was worse! So right then and there I made a promise to myself:

Alex, you're going to learn something from this. All you want to do is play soccer, but you can't do that right now.

This injury is going to teach you to deal with disappointment and make the best of it. And it's going to show you how to overcome adversity. This is going to make you a stronger person.

When Setbacks Happen, Take Care of Yourself

When you have a setback, it's important to stop and take stock of the situation. That's what I had to do so that I wouldn't freak out about my ACL. Don't forget to breathe, and don't forget that, as I said above, this isn't the end of the world. Most of all, take care of yourself— talk to a friend, go to the movies, have a hot chocolate, or whatever you need to do to make yourself feel better in that moment when you're feeling your worst. Taking care of yourself *will* make you feel better, and then you'll be able to rearrange your goals, or if necessary, figure out new ones.

CHAPTER 7

When I injured my ACL, my mom was working as a pharmaceutical rep. Her job required her to know a lot of doctors—by reputation and personally—so she made it her mission to find me a top-notch surgeon. After a lot of pushing and shoving, she got me in with Dr. Neal ElAttrache, who was the best doctor in LA for knee and shoulder injuries. He squeezed me into his schedule thanks to Mom. I'll always thank her for that, because Dr. ElAttrache was *amazing*.

Dr. ElAttrache was in high demand. One time in the waiting room I even saw Travis Barker from Blink-182! I remember thinking, *Mom got me in with a really good doctor*. Dr. ElAttrache was so nice and really took time with me, focusing on what I needed.

My surgery was scheduled for early morning not long after my injury. My dad drove me to the hospital at four a.m., and we were both very sleepy and nervous. But as I headed into surgery, my dad couldn't have been more reassuring.

"You'll see me in just a few hours." Dad kissed me on the head and then waved good-bye as I was wheeled into the operating room. I'd never had surgery before, and I was a little scared. But Dr. ElAttrache had talked me through it, so I felt prepared.

I was given anesthesia, and I felt myself drifting off. Before I knew it, I was back in the recovery room, with Dad by my side. If you've never had surgery before, I'm telling you, it's the weirdest thing to wake up and not know where you are. You feel like you *just* went into the operating room, and then, boom, you're out after what feels like three seconds, lying in a bed in a strange, sterile recovery room. Of course, my surgery had lasted for about two hours, but it seemed like it was over in the blink of an eye.

My parents had been waiting for me to wake up. "Everything went well, Alex," said my dad with the sweetest look on his face. In case you haven't seen my dad, he's kind of a manly man, with bushy eyebrows and a big beard. But he has these very kind, gentle eyes that speak volumes. Right then they were telling me how much he loved me. "We'll be going home very soon."

And we did. We were in the car pretty much immediately after I stopped feeling groggy.

I didn't play with a team for five more months, which was one of the hardest things I've ever experienced. I'd never gone that long without playing, and I was an emotional wreck a lot of the time. Luckily, my family was so supportive. My current and former teammates called or sent me messages all the time, wishing me a speedy recovery. I did physical therapy three times a week, and I was dedicated to it. I never slacked off and never missed a session, and I always did the exercises I was supposed to do at home. If you have an injury and you want it to get better, you have to be committed. After I finished PT, I would watch my Cypress teammates practice. I knew I would never play with them again, but I was the captain, and I wasn't going to quit before the end. Again, I was dedicated—on and off the field.

I was forced to do a lot of sitting around, too, which was unusual for me. I had been on the go for so long that just relaxing, watching TV or reading, felt strange. I think a lot of us who have big goals never truly allow ourselves to rest. I don't want to call us overachievers—that implies you're doing something wrong—but for people who do a lot, *not* doing a lot is tough. After surgery, I had to let that go, and while it wasn't easy, it ultimately paid off because it allowed me to recover.

Within a few months, I started running in physical therapy. I took it slowly at first, then got faster and faster till I felt I was almost back up to speed. I also began practicing on the field while wearing a knee brace. I pushed myself hard, but I knew my limits. I persuaded my therapists to let me do more and more, and they responded, allowing me to do things as long as they weren't a danger to me. I was so worried about reinjuring myself, but I knew that keeping active was important to healing, so I forced myself to get out and about.

I think it actually took me longer to recover emotionally than it did to heal physically. Like I said, I was back on the field in five months, which is *fast* for an ACL injury, and while I wasn't physically 100 percent, I could see the light at the end of the tunnel. But it took almost a year to feel the same confidence and aggressiveness I had before. I was so worried about being injured again and losing ground as a player. I'd always been so good, so not being as good as I wanted to be right out of the gate was crushing. And I felt I'd missed so much in those months I was away from my teams, especially the Diamond Bar High School varsity team. I'd played with them for four years, and I had to miss the end of my senior season. But I realized I just had to let that go. You can't change the past; you can only accept it for what it is. In the end, I think I finally recovered emotionally because I realized that my injury was just a bump in the road, and eventually, I saw myself improve from where I'd been before. I showed myself that being sidelined wasn't going to stop me.

I can't say for certain, but I have a theory about why

my ACL got torn. I think my body just wasn't ready for the stress I was putting on it. I'd had a few minor quad and hamstring injuries prior to tearing my ACL, so I hadn't been training every day. With my muscles unable to fully recover, my joints just weren't prepared for intense exercise and weren't equipped to deal with that other injury.

With proper training, I believe you can decrease your chances of becoming injured like I did, and that's why I've worked with FIFA's Sports Injury Prevention Program. They recommend a series of exercises that will help warm up your muscles. They emphasize balance, flexibility, and a small amount of noncontact running so that you're physically prepared when you go on the field. I warm up like this every single time I play—whether it's practice, scrimmages, or the World Cup final—and I can tell it's helped prevent further injuries. My knee still hurts sometimes, but I've never again torn my ACL.

In early 2012, I went back to Diamond Bar High School to help coach the varsity team for a day. It was so much fun. I was still a Brahma (our mascot) at heart, so being back on the field I'd played on so many times felt like being home. In practice, we jogged together, I showed the players how to take penalty shots, and we did a few passing drills.

But one of the most meaningful moments was

meeting a senior player named Stevie Thomas, who'd been injured and couldn't practice with us. She'd strained the outside of her right knee and had been sidelined for a few games. I taught her how to warm up and threw in a few more tips. I can always relate to players who've been sidelined, especially with ACL injuries. It's a very emotional thing to go through when soccer is all you know.

What she said afterward made it all worthwhile. "Because Alex went through a similar thing," she said, "I know I'll be able to do it too."

You may have been injured playing a sport you love, but remember, it doesn't have to happen again. Do the necessary steps to prepare yourself, and your body and mind can be strong and injury-free. If you're worried about being sidelined from an activity you love for whatever reason—illness or having to focus on something else in your life—just work hard in advance so that you'll never feel too far behind. Preparation is key to getting ahead *and* not falling behind.

During the Tough Times, Focus on Your Passion
The disruption of a goal can be one of the best things that ever happened to you. For me, being injured and staying off the field reminded me of what my true passion was: soccer. If I'd kept playing without interruption, I might have never had the time to sit back and fully

realize the deep, wonderful love I have for the sport. They say "absence makes the heart grow fonder," and that's the case when I'm off the field. If something gets in the way of your pursuit of a goal, let that be a time to reflect upon and truly embrace that passion.

CHAPTER 8

The months leading up to college were hard in some ways but easy in others. I was still recovering from my ACL injury, so I felt emotionally drained, but I was so excited about college that my happiness helped alleviate the tough times.

Leaving for college may be years ahead for you, but it's like any other transition. It's an incredibly emotional time, but it can also be one of the best times of your life. Try not to view it as an ending—it's really a new beginning. If you're close with your high school friends, you'll stay close. Some of my high school teammates are still my best friends in the world! And you're going to meet so many new people in college, have new adventures, and learn more than you ever have before. You have *so* much to look forward to.

The prospect of being on your own in college can be thrilling—I certainly felt that way at times. But I also felt lucky that I wasn't really saying good-bye to my parents. My dad was still planning to travel to all my games, so I knew I'd see him a lot. Still, I cherished the times I got to spend with him late in my senior year.

As you know, my dad loves a good game, especially when he's challenging his daughters. In California, you really need a car to get around, so when my sisters and I were sixteen, we got used cars. There was no way my parents were going to trust us with something brand-new! In fact, I rear-ended someone about six months after I got my license. Ugh. But when we got a little older and were about to leave home, Dad devised a strategy where we'd each get to pick a new car for college based on sort of a points system. We'd get points if we made certain accomplishments or met our goals.

My dad said, "By your last semester of high school, we'll count up all of your grades, extracurricular activities, sports, charity work, and everything that you're doing that helps shape your future. The final tally will count toward a new car."

I took the challenge on as my own personal mission. Having a target to hit was exciting to me. But I wasn't just going to meet my goal. I was going to exceed it, and then some.

"Challenge accepted, Dad!"

Jenny and Jeri had been put up to this years before me. Jenny was a good student, so she made lots of As, and before the end of high school she picked out a Mercury:

a nice, sensible car. Jeri was a good student and loved cheerleading, so she made the squad, got good grades, and picked out a Chevy truck. It was as hardworking as she was.

But I wasn't to be stopped. I scored so many goals that year that I left my sisters in the dust, and I picked out a Lexus 350. I think my parents actually let me do this because I'd gotten a scholarship to pay for college. Otherwise, there's no way they would have agreed to it!

My dad and I flew to Phoenix to pick it up, and we planned to drive it back. I have such good memories of us together on this trip, and my dad, always the coach, used it as a time to teach me lessons.

As we pulled up into a fast-food restaurant on the way home, he said, "Okay, now here's a whole parking lot. Where do you park your brand-new car? Do you drive it in this slot between two cars? Do you put it in a spot where there aren't really any cars around, or do you go to this corner where there's a car on one side and a divider on the other?"

I responded, "I'd park it where no other cars are parked."

"Wrong!" he said. "You put it where there's a divider because then only one car can park on the side of you. You don't know when the lot's going to fill up and there are going to be two cars next to you. You don't know if someone's going to hit you, but you reduce your chances if you have a divider on one side."

I imagine my dad saw this trip as a way to have some special time with me before I left for college. I was the last kid to leave the house, and he was looking ahead to an empty nest. When you leave for college, for summer camp, or any time away from home, don't forget that while you may be overcome with feelings—excitement, nervousness, or even ambivalence—your parents probably are too. You may be really ready to leave them, but those memories of the last few months can be important ones. They certainly were for me and Dad.

Like me, my dad isn't overtly emotional. We're both sensitive, but we don't really wear our hearts on our sleeves. In a house with four talkative girls—me, my two sisters, and my mom—he never really says much during family conversations. He's learned to be a guy who kind of sits back and speaks up when he has something to say. He and I don't need to express ourselves on an emotional basis, and that's why we get each other. Soccer has become a way to show our feelings to each other.

This all couldn't have been more evident than when he dropped me off at the airport the day I left for Cal. Because I was going to see him in a few weeks, there wasn't a huge buildup to me leaving. I was actually surprised he even parked the car and walked me to the ticket desk!

When we walked into the airport, I saw one of my future teammates, Megan Jesolva, who is still one of my closest friends. There she was, crying, hugging her family, and kissing everyone. I laughed, thinking how different we were. My dad just checked my bags, looked at me, and said, "Okay, Al. See you in a few weeks."

And I was off.

In Times of Transition, No Feeling Is Wrong

Like I said before, leaving for college can be exciting, challenging, heartbreaking, or all of the above. But those emotions aren't just reserved for college—they can come up at any time of transition: changing schools, moving, or breaking up with a boyfriend. Or you may be like me— you might not feel a certain change is such a big deal! No matter how you feel, it's totally normal. No emotion is "right" or "wrong." Just focus on the fact that you're moving forward toward your goals, and that's exciting in and of itself.

CHAPTER 9

I'd traveled a lot in high school—weekend tournaments here and there, sometimes with my parents and sometimes without them—but I'd never been away from home for as long as I was going to be now that I was in college. UC Berkeley is four hundred miles from Diamond Bar—a good six-hour drive—so while I was going to see my parents pretty often, it wasn't like I would be coming home on weekends. And being in Berkeley was going to be *so* different from Diamond Bar. I'd grown up in a nice, somewhat conservative suburb; Berkeley was a bohemian mecca that embraced politics and social causes. As for the weather? I brought lots of sweaters. It felt like it was always in the eighties in Diamond Bar. In Berkeley, the winters were going to be cool and wet and the summers were going to be in the midseventies. Granted, it was warmer than a lot of the rest of the country, but to me that was chilly!

I'd wanted a change, and that's why I chose Cal. I think getting out of your comfort zone can be a really good thing. You may love your hometown and your family, but I bet you'll love it more if you get away from it for a bit. As I said before, absence often makes the heart grow fonder. Or if you hate where you're from, moving away from it will allow you to grow as an individual, and you won't be in the shadow of your family and childhood forever.

I've always believed that education happens outside the classroom as much as inside it. Being in Berkeley was going to be an education—all the cultural events, restaurants, shops, and different kinds of people, not just on campus, but in the town. True, I'd be on the soccer field for hours a day, but I loved the idea of being in a place as diverse as Berkeley, California. And it was so close to San Francisco—just a quick ride on the BART (Bay Area Rapid Transportation). No more LA traffic!

My excitement wasn't just reserved for my social life, though. I couldn't wait to start playing soccer. But just before my first practice, I got a huge surprise: The head coach had left the school. Standing on the field was an entirely new coach, along with an assistant coach who was out of *her* comfort zone with a new head coach, and a plan for the team that was dramatically different from what I'd thought I was signing up for. I can't say I was upset or shocked—I had nothing to compare this to— but many of my teammates were.

Our new coach was named Neil McGuire, and he'd just come from Texas Tech, where he'd also been head coach. He was Scottish by birth and still had his accent. Have you ever watched soccer on TV with a British commentator? Soccer always sounds better in a British accent (so does everything!), so you just assume they know more about the game than an American commentator. That was Neil for us that day. He stated his goal right away: He wanted us to win the NCAA championship. We'd made it to the second round the year before, but this year he wanted us to win it. I liked his ambition immediately. I dreamed big, so I loved having a coach who did too.

While the season started off well, I sprained my ankle early on and had to miss four games. I was out for three weeks, which felt like a lifetime and was such a blow to me. How was I going to get better and better at soccer and reach my goal of becoming a professional athlete if I kept getting injured? The memory of my torn ACL was all too fresh in my mind.

Watching my new team from the sidelines, though, I learned so much. Rather than focusing primarily on what *I* was doing—*Were my passes good? Did I gain control of the ball enough?*—I could pay attention to how the team worked. If I'd been on the field, I would have been in my own head. On the sidelines, I felt like I could soak in what other players were doing.

Watching the team interact helped me plot my strategy for how I was going to be a valuable contributor to the Bears during my first season. I wanted to be the team's best scorer. It was just like my dad had taught me—in any game, you have an option: to win or to lose. I chose to win.

Expect the Unexpected

The last thing I expected when I got to Cal was that there would be a new head coach. But that's life! Just when you think you know what the future holds, it suddenly changes. You may have made lists, plans, charts, whatever, thinking you know *exactly* the route to achieving your dreams. But then something happens, and you have to adjust. As you're making plans and figuring out the path toward your dreams, just accept that things might not go smoothly. But that doesn't mean you won't get where you want to go. The path to success is often crooked, and there may be roadblocks along the way, but you can get around them.

CHAPTER 10

One of the most important things that happened to me my freshman year didn't happen on the field or in the classroom. It happened when I reconnected with someone I'd met briefly through friends the year before on my spring break—a male soccer player named Servando Carrasco.

Raised in Mexico and San Diego, Servando was a year older than me but only a semester ahead of me at Cal. This was because he'd spent part of the previous year in Argentina playing semiprofessional soccer, attempting to sign professionally. He'd been considering signing a contract when he got a call from his mother in San Diego. She told him she had advanced-stage breast cancer, and he was faced with a huge decision: to stay and pursue his dreams or to go and help his beloved mom. Servando got on the next flight home. He was with his mom when she had chemo and a mastectomy, and he helped nurse her back to good health.

Servando wanted to stay close to his mom, so he

decided not to go back to South America and instead signed with Cal in January 2007. Like I said, I met him briefly on my spring break in April 2007, but when I arrived at Cal we got back in touch.

We hit it off immediately and started spending time together. And as I got to know him better as a friend, things accelerated quickly; we were dating within a month. I felt so comfortable with him, and I loved his friends. I was practically a fourth roommate at his apartment, like I was just one of the guys. We shared a love of soccer, had the same values, and enjoyed doing the same things for fun. I admired his devotion to his mom so much, and while I wasn't there while she was battling breast cancer, part of the reason I still wear a pink headband during games is to honor her and other survivors.

I realized how serious things were between me and Servando while I was at the NCAA tournament my freshman year. The night before we were set to play Stanford, I was talking to one of my teammates.

"I feel really strongly about this guy," I said. "I can't stop thinking about him."

And sure enough, Servando showed up at the game without me even asking him to. I'd been missing him the whole trip, and all the while he'd been planning to drive from Cal to Palo Alto to watch us play. I think that was the turning point of our relationship.

Wow. This guy is amazing, I thought. *I think I really love him.*

We've been together ever since, and in fact, we just got married! But more on that later. . . .

When I got back on my feet and began playing again after my injury, I hit the ground running. Literally. I became the go-to girl for scoring early during my freshman year because I could outrun so many players, and my shots were often dead-on. This wasn't just luck—it was something I'd practiced time and again.

In late September, we played against Saint Mary's, a Catholic college located about ten miles from Oakland. This was my first game after my injury, and I did something our team hadn't done since 2004: I scored a hat trick. For those of you who don't know, a hat trick is scoring three goals in one game. It doesn't happen all that much for a player, but when it does, it's so much fun.

I accomplished a few other feats I was very proud of that year. I scored the game-winning goal against Santa Clara University, who had been undefeated that season, and I was named Pac-10 and Soccer America's Player of the Week—in the same week. I think it would have been easy to feel like everything was going so well *if* I'd chosen to think only about myself. But I was on a team, and when you're part of something like that, everyone's happiness rests on everyone's shoulders.

That fall, one of our goalkeepers, another freshman named Jorden LaFontaine-Kussmann, was diagnosed with lymphoma. Jorden was one of my roommates, so we were close. After she was diagnosed, she stayed in Berkeley, so I saw her just as often, but she had to undergo several rounds of chemotherapy. The entire men's varsity team shaved their heads to support her, and we all wore wristbands that read *JLK*. Thankfully, Jorden's okay now, but we were all so scared for her then.

I'll talk about this more later in the book, but Jorden's cancer wasn't an isolated incident. Lots of goalkeepers and soccer players are coming down with blood cancers like lymphoma now, and it's believed to be linked to artificial turf. So not only was her illness a wake-up call for me, but it was also the first incident I'd seen in what's become a very frightening pattern.

That season, Jorden said something that really struck me, which was that she was viewing being out as "just being injured for six months." I thought, *I'd been injured almost six months, and it had just been my knee. Not cancer.* When you see someone you're so close with go through something like she was, it really puts everything in perspective. Suddenly your problems feel so small. Suddenly you feel very thankful for what you have. I think you have to feel that every day, not just on the days when you see something awful happen. Gratitude is so important, and I try to be thankful for my life every day.

The NCAA tournament—what we'd all been working for and what our coach had set in his sights for us to win—rolled around that November. We beat Santa Clara in the first game. They never scored, and we were dominant the entire game. But then we played Stanford in the second round.

We were down 1–0 until the game was almost over, and then I made a goal with 1:50 left in regulation, sending us into overtime. Perhaps this is where I first got my reputation as a late-game threat. I scored in the last minutes then, and I've been doing it ever since.

Both teams were scoreless at the end of both periods of overtime, which sent us into penalty kicks. Unfortunately, we lost on kicks, but we were proud of how we'd played. And my final goal meant that I scored more goals that year than any other Cal player—as a freshman.

It was a season of highs and lows, but I was optimistic. I knew the following season would be our year.

Be Thankful

I mentioned earlier how important gratitude is. But I think it's important not just to be grateful for the people and material possessions in your life, but also to be thankful when you accomplish one of your goals. At the end of my freshman season at Cal, I stopped, took stock of my year, and let myself be happy for a good season. I mentally thanked my coach, my teammates, and myself. Internalizing that gratitude made the accomplishments feel ever richer, and it will do the same for you.

CHAPTER 11

During the spring semester of my freshman year, I was called up to the US women's national under-20 team for training. U-20 is a team operated under US Soccer, the governing body of soccer in the United States. U-20's purpose is to train girls in preparation for playing on the national team. You're not guaranteed to get on the national team if you're on U-20, but it's a big stepping stone if you're headed in that direction.

My achievements as a college athlete coupled with my experience on the U-17 team had made the coaches notice me. Still, getting called up felt like a huge accomplishment. I had worked hard for it, and I knew it was all a part of my path to becoming a professional athlete, so I was thrilled.

Unfortunately, I performed horribly at the training camp, which was held in Los Angeles at the StubHub Center. I was nervous the whole time, and I fumbled practices and scrimmages in a way I never had before. I hadn't played on a national team since before my ACL injury, when I'd played on the U-17 team, so I think I was just rusty. Couple that with my nerves, and you had a recipe for disaster.

I left training with a pit in my stomach. *Maybe I'm just not cut out for this*, I thought. I was happy to go back to Cal—I'd missed games and practices with them—but I couldn't shake the unhappiness I felt about doing so badly during training. I knew I wouldn't be called for the upcoming U-20 World Cup, so my dreams had been dashed. And it was all my fault.

But soon a miracle happened. One of the U-20 players who had been chosen had to drop off the team, and I took her spot for the World Cup qualifying tournament. I was literally the last player added to the team. I mentally thanked the coaches. *Thank you for believing in me and giving me a second chance.*

Sometimes life is like that. You can do badly, but you're granted a reprieve. I don't think you can count on things like that happening, but when they do, feel grateful and make the most of them. I was beyond grateful—I was ecstatic. And I vowed to play the best soccer of my life because of it.

Every other year, the culmination of U-20's season is the World Cup (not the one you see on TV, but the youth

World Cup). You might not have even realized there's a U-20 World Cup, but there is, and believe me, we are just as competitive as our older teammates! Plus, it's exciting that our World Cup is every two years rather than every four.

When I started playing with the U-20, the team was still sort of reeling from a terrible fourth-place finish in the 2006 FIFA U-20 Women's World Championship. They had lost on penalty kicks in the semifinal round, then on penalty kicks in the third-place game. They'd had a full season between that loss and when I started, but it was still in the back of people's minds.

We had to travel to Mexico for the qualifying tournament, which was held in June. Unfortunately, we lost to Canada 1–0 in the qualification finals, but with a second-place finish, we still advanced to the U-20 World Cup. We felt good, and we knew the best was yet to come.

Before we headed to the World Cup, which was going to be held in Chile in late November, I did a little more traveling with the U-20 team. We were in England for a few days, and then I went back to school for my sophomore year. My head was spinning a little bit from all the travel, but I had to remind myself that this was fun, not work. Yes, I was working—hard—but I couldn't lose sight of the fact that this was my dream.

I think sometimes we fall into patterns where we chase a goal so hard that it becomes drudgery. Or something requires so much time and effort that it stops feeling fun. I planned my wedding for most of 2014, and I felt that way constantly! Which is crazy. I scolded myself. *It's a wedding, not the SAT. It's supposed to be fun.* That year in the run-up to the U-20 World Cup, I had to tell myself that all the time. And it helped—reminding myself of how much I loved my goals made them feel fun again.

Early-season play with Cal was great too. It was liberating to be back on the field with my school. I loved being a Bear. I kept up my reputation as a late-game scorer, getting a terrific last-minute goal in the 3–1 win season opener against San Jose State, for example. But after nailing nine goals for my team, I had to leave for Portland to train for the U-20 World Cup.

This time I was accompanied by one of my Cal teammates, Megan Jesolva, who was the leader in assists on the Bears. And yes, she was the same person I'd seen at the airport the day I left for college! She and I had become so close freshman year. We went to San Francisco together all the time, we studied together, and we hung around with the same group of guys from the men's soccer team at Cal, including Servando. We had a similar sense of ambition—both of us wanted to play professional soccer—so we just *got* each other. I was thrilled to have her with me.

Training began, and we played some friendly, or exhibition, games against Canada before traveling to Chile for the tournament. It's funny they call them friendly games—Canada had beaten us in the qualifying tournament, so they were more competition than friends! But that's how soccer works. Your supposed enemy may become your training partner in the next game. And my teammates on the U-20 team, whom I valued more than anything, were my competitors in other games because they played for rival colleges. Megan was the only person on the team who was my teammate on both squads.

Friendly games are good training for a season or for tournament play. Coaches use them to see where the threats are in the other teams and what they need to pay attention to on their own teams. It's sort of like preseason football—it doesn't determine if you're going to go to the Super Bowl, but it does help give the league, players, coaches, and fans the lay of the land.

These early games would also determine who was on the starting roster for the World Cup. And even though I was picked last for the team, I was going to be a starter if it killed me. I'd played hard against Canada, and I worked my tail off in practices. And at the end of October, our coach, Tony DiCicco, announced that I was one of the starting forwards.

I couldn't believe it—I'd accomplished a major goal. I was going to Chile as a starter. I was nineteen years old, and I was going to play in the World Cup.

Don't Make Opponents into Enemies

When you're going after your goals, you'll have people stand in your way. When we lost the NCAA tournament my freshman year, there were players on other teams who'd tripped me, prevented me from scoring, given me dirty looks, and frustrated my play so much that I felt defeated. These same players became my teammates on the U-20 team. The lesson here is that you can't view an opponent—someone who, at one moment, prevents you from reaching your goals—as a sworn enemy. For one thing, the unfortunate truth is you'll meet people like that throughout your life, and there's no point wasting your energy on them. Also, they might be your partner in the next game (or group partner or coworker), and you'll need them! So don't hold grudges or be petty. Maturity and good sportsmanship will reward you and help you when you're going after your dreams.

CHAPTER 12

Chile had put its heart and soul into the U-20 Women's World Cup that year, and it showed. It's true that this wasn't an event people would be watching on TV around the world. Women's soccer is a big draw, but at the U-20 level, it's not on everyone's radar. But you wouldn't have known that if you'd landed in Santiago when we did.

The Chilean government had rebuilt four stadiums for the tournament and had worked hard to drum up local support, and fans had responded immediately. In South America, men's soccer is the big draw, but we had packed stadiums for this tournament, and it made all the difference. I really felt like we were on the world stage.

We played France and Argentina in our first two games. Our game against France was a big win, 3–0, and our match with Argentina was a crushing defeat for them, also 3–0. I scored two goals against Argentina, one in the ninetieth minute. There I was again—the late-game scorer.

If you don't know anything about soccer in Argentina, I will sum it up in one word: MASSIVE. The most famous men's player from there, Lionel Messi, is such a big international star that he's appearing in American commercials now. I love his team in the Spanish league, Barcelona, and I have tremendous respect for how the Argentine national team nurtured him as a player. Unfortunately, that doesn't translate to the women's side, where other women's sports are much bigger. I think that's a shame. We US women are lucky. Since 1999, soccer has been a big deal for girls, and we don't stand in the shadow of boys. If anything, we are more famous and more successful—look at Mia Hamm! But it's different in Argentina.

The tables turned on us in our final game in the group stage, against China, and they beat us 2–0. But no matter—our wins against France and Argentina had secured us a spot in the tournament's quarterfinals, where we were set to play England.

We won against England, 3–0. Boom! That was our third shutout game of the tournament.

The semifinal was a little tighter—we beat Germany 1–0 after an early-game goal against them. And then it was on to the final. It was my first major international final, and we were set to play North Korea, the team who'd won the previous U-20 World Cup. Historically, they hadn't always been the most challenging team, but lately they'd been great, and their 2006 win in the U-20 finals had confirmed that.

The final started off at a furious pace, and we were constantly getting pressure from Korea. Even when my teammate Sydney Leroux scored from way outside the penalty box in the twenty-third minute, we didn't feel completely at ease.

I had really gotten to know Sydney over the last few months. She played for UCLA, so I was familiar with her from Pac-10 play and had gone against her in many games, but playing with her as my teammate was a whole different ball game. Since those first few months together, we've gotten so close. She's now on the national team, and we've gone cliff diving on vacation in Hawaii and dressed up together for two Halloweens in a row. Sydney was also just at my wedding.

But back to the game. Like I said, we were playing so well, but a 1–0 margin felt a little too slight. We wanted a comfortable lead going into halftime.

With three minutes left in the half, my teammate Elli Reed threw the ball in from the right sideline, and I gained control of it. Caught between two defenders, I dribbled past them. I almost lost the ball to yet another, but I got control and took off. Another

Korean defender came after me, and I cut inside and passed her. I was twenty-six yards from the goal, but I saw my shot, and I took it. I kicked hard with my left foot, and the ball sailed long . . . and over the goalkeeper's head. It went into the upper-left corner of the goal. We were up 2–0!

I was later quoted as saying that making that goal was one of the best feelings of my life, and I still feel that way. Not only was it the sheer exhilaration of seeing it go in, but it was also the fact that I wasn't intending to make the shot that way. I'd gotten off-balance just before I kicked, so I was kind of surprised. I'd been hoping just to get the ball into the goal, but when I wobbled, it sailed perfectly toward the far post and went in. I made a shot in a way I hadn't necessarily meant to.

Halftime came and went, and then we went into the second half. But the game stayed ours.

We finished off the match strong, winning 2–1. The North Koreans netted a goal in the ninety-second minute, but it was too late. The referee blew the whistle almost immediately after they scored.

I could hardly believe it. We'd won the U-20 World Cup, and we'd done it because of hard work and sheer determination. I had accomplished a goal I'd held for so long, that I'd dreamed about so many times. But that night I dared to dream one more thing: I wanted to join the US women's national team, and I wanted us to win the World Cup, too.

Maybe I was feeling that way not just because of the way I'd played but also because a seed had been planted. Pia Sundhage, the head coach of the women's national team, had been in the stands watching the U-20 team that day. I wonder now what would have happened if she hadn't been there. Would I have been called up to the national team when I was? Did her being there that day change my future forever? I'll never know, but I do know that I'm so glad the final played out the way it did. I think we really impressed her that day, and I know that my playing well gave her something to think about.

People Are Watching

If you're pursuing your goals successfully, people will start paying attention. It could be the teacher who notices how hard you're studying and wants to write you a recommendation for a summer program, or it could be the varsity coach who sees that terrific shot you made in a junior varsity basketball game. Pia Sundhage had taken notice of me at some point, and that might have contributed to her decision to come to the finals of the U-20 World Cup. The lesson here is that you should always try your best because it may attract the attention of someone influential who wants to help you along the path to your dreams.

CHAPTER 13

Things were just a little more serious for me when I got home. I was getting called for interviews and was being recognized on campus more often. It was beginning to dawn on me that my dream of playing soccer professionally—the goal I'd had since I'd scrawled it on a piece of paper when I was eight—might actually come true. In fact, it looked like chances were good that it would, and soon.

That summer, the Cal team traveled around Europe, playing exhibition games. We played in Milan, Lake Como, Rome, Switzerland, and Ireland. It was an absolute whirlwind, but I had the time of my life. We were in games with players from around the world, which, of course, I'd experienced before, but it was a first for many of my teammates. Italian players play differently from Americans, and so do Irish and Swiss players. The sport has reached so many countries that it's evolved in tiny ways in each corner of the world. That doesn't mean there aren't the same rules—FIFA ensures that the game is pretty consistent across the globe—but there are nuances of play that make each country's players different.

Soccer has given me the opportunity to travel the world. I realize I've been lucky—you may play on a team that doesn't venture outside your own state. But if you have any opportunity to travel outside the country, do it. You can learn so much from other cultures—the foods they eat, the languages they speak, their belief systems, their traditions, and more. Even reading a book about another country or watching a foreign film will teach you a lot. However you do it, getting a taste of something outside your own comfort zone may change your perspective on life.

I dove even further into the world outside my home when I traveled to Madrid, Spain, for a month that summer to study. Ever since my sister Jeri studied abroad in Australia, I'd dreamed about doing the same. I spoke Spanish very well, but I wasn't fluent, and I wanted to be more conversant. A month in Spain would help me do that.

I loved every second of my month there. The trip also reminded me how much I enjoyed learning outside the soccer field. Academics were still so important to me. As I mentioned before, I'd decided long before college that there was no way I was going to neglect my studies for soccer. I was about to declare my major: political economy, with a concentration on Latin America, which meant taking four semesters of Spanish. I worked hard while I was in Madrid so I could become fluent. But I also had a lot of fun. After focusing on soccer so much for so long, I think I desperately needed to let loose. We ate tapas, danced, traveled to other cities on the weekends, and watched some fantastic soccer. And after the month was over, I returned home fluent—or close, at least!

By the time I returned to the States, I was ready to be back on the field. I missed soccer desperately—my love of it lives way down deep in my bones—and I was itching to go back to my team. But Spain was a fantastic end to a school year that had given me so much: the World Cup, a loving boyfriend, and real hope that I was going to fulfill my dreams. I was ready to do even more great things in my junior year.

Step Out of Your World

When you're going after your goals, you can sometimes become set in your ways. You might wear the same lucky socks every game or eat the same breakfast before every game, or more broadly speaking, just develop the same mind-set before every big challenge or step. But venturing outside your comfort zone can be really good for you. Exploring other cultures is so important, whether you do it on vacation or by reading a book. I learned things from playing against Italians that made my game better. Don't get into a rut. Constantly try to expand your world view so you can dive into your goals with a well-rounded mentality.

CHAPTER 14

I 'd been away so much during my sophomore year, training and playing with the U-20 team—plus the World Cup had booked me solid for weeks at a time—so I just hadn't been the presence on my college team that I knew I'd be this year. With that in mind, I was excited and ready when I started preseason training in August. I wanted to give Cal my all during my junior year.

I got some good news midway through the month. I'd been put on the short list for the Hermann Trophy, which is the biggest individual player award in college soccer, and the winner was going to be decided later that year by Division I soccer head coaches. My coach, Neil, couldn't have been more complimentary of me when I got named. He thought I'd worked for it and that I deserved it, and that meant the world to me.

We'd all gotten a lot closer to Neil on the European trip. In fact, we'd all gotten a lot closer to one another— for the first time in a long while, we'd had a chance to

talk about life, our families, our boyfriends, and everything in between. We weren't rushing off to class or hus-
tling on the field. Instead, we were bonding in a beautiful
place. But getting to know Neil as a person was beneficial
to us and to him. It's one thing for your team to feel
like they're together, but it's the icing on the cake when
you're unified with your coach. Neil had been our coach
for three years, but this was the first year it truly felt like
home with him.

This was a good thing because we had two new assistant coaches. Our old assistant coach, Jennifer Thomas,
had left the previous year, which had been tough for us.
She was a rock for our team, and she really understood
the Cal program because she'd been a player there herself. But we were lucky to get two new assistant coaches
who seemed very promising. One of them, Tracy Hamm,
had been a Cal player too. We needed someone who
was instantly part of our culture, and she fit the bill. The
other new coach, Libby Hassett, was incredibly skilled at
technique, which was something we'd needed to work
on. Her plan was to help our goalkeepers zero in on the
specifics that would prevent balls getting across the line.
The previous year, a lot of shots on goal had gone in
when they just shouldn't have. Libby was also so funny,
always making jokes and keeping things light. She obviously knew when to get serious, but she just loved to

mess around, make fun of herself, and keep any situation happy. I loved her work-hard, play-hard attitude.

With the new assistant coaches, Neil had pretty big ambitions for us that year. The team had been so dependent on a few players to hold us together—and I was one of them—but he wanted to strengthen each and every player to make us stronger as team. This extended to the ten new freshmen on the team, whom Neil vowed to push harder than the rest of us. He realized that two or three players can't hold a whole team together, so he wanted each of us to play our best that year. This could lead us to winning the Pac-10 championship and advancing beyond the second round in the NCAA tournament. We'd been so close in the past, especially in my freshman year, when we'd lost to Stanford on penalty kicks.

We really put our best foot forward in those early games—we had a few shutouts, we consistently outshot our opponents, and our defense was stronger than it had ever been. I scored a hat trick in one game, which was thrilling. The early results showed how hard we'd worked. We rose to #7 in the national rankings, which made us all proud.

I have so many theories why the beginning of that season was such a good one, but I think what I'll remember most is that we were like sisters. Maybe it was coming off that summer trip to Europe, or maybe it was having two new coaches, which can cause you to either sink or swim. But our team stuck together like glue, which made our game all the better.

I was thankful we had this camaraderie because things were about to get rocky, and if there was anything we were going to need, it was one another.

Become a Mentor

When I was a junior, I'd had national team experience and had gone to two NCAA tournaments, plus a World Cup final. I had loads of experience under my belt, yet I realized how important it was to be a good role model to the underclassmen, especially the freshmen, who had just come in. When you're going after your goals, you may spend a lot of time looking up to people—coaches, teachers, or players you respect—but don't forget how important it is to *be* a mentor. If you take the time to help someone improve their game or work harder toward their goals, you'll probably discover that you learn something too. People who are successful often become more successful because they're good teachers and role models, so don't hesitate to take someone under your wing.

CHAPTER 15

We lost a heartbreaking game midway through the season. Despite outshooting them 25–8, we were defeated by Cal Poly 1–0 in overtime—our first overtime loss of the season. The game really wore us out, and we dropped in the rankings. None of us felt good about it.

It's one thing to lose a game when you've fought like crazy, but it's another to lose a game you're supposed to win. You just feel lousy when that happens. This isn't reserved to soccer, of course. I've felt like a failure after making a bad grade on a test that I knew I should have aced. It's okay to let it get you down. But don't let it keep you down. After all, it's just one day. Things can turn around, but you have to be able to put the effort in. That definitely won't happen if you're spending all your time moping around!

A week after that loss, we were still trying to get out of our funk when one of the worst things a team can go through happened. Neil just up and left us.

We were in the locker room at halftime during a game against Sacramento State, and no one was happy. We were down 1–0 against a team we were expected to beat, and despite taking more shots than our opponent, we just couldn't get on the board. As we were staring at the whiteboard waiting for halftime instructions, Neil came in the back door and just stood there for a split second, looking as if he had no intention of moving to the front of the room.

"This isn't working for me. I'm out," he yelled. And without further explanation, he turned his back on us and left.

To say we were shocked would be an understatement. We were in utter disbelief, and we were crushed. I looked around the locker room and saw mouths wide open, and I felt tears of rage coming to my eyes. A few of my team-mates burst into tears. I thought, *How could he do this to us? Why is he leaving?*

What made me so upset, in part, was that he didn't offer any explanation. In my family, you talk things through and stick together. You don't just leave. We were a team, and we'd just started to feel that Neil was part of our sisterhood. And now he was leaving us when we were at our lowest?

I was a team leader, and I felt I had to hold it together, especially for my younger teammates. We needed to win this game, so I disguised my fears and attempted to motivate my team. We had to move on. We still had another half to play against Sacramento State.

But we couldn't get past our anger and grief. We lost 1–0 in a stinging, painful defeat. We were just too overcome with emotion to play our best soccer.

I went back to my room and logged on to Twitter. My fingers were flying as I typed:

You turned your back on us once. we can and will turn our backs on you for good.

You are not welcome back.

I'd always been so mature and so diplomatic, but what Neil had done was beyond the pale. I wanted to scream and cry, and I needed to let my emotions out. I wanted everyone to know how hurt I felt—and how devastated my whole team was.

We live in the social media age, when it's really easy to post every single one of your thoughts online. It makes you feel better for a little bit because you get lots of immediate support from other people—thumbs-up and comments on Facebook or retweets on Twitter—but it may not make you feel better in the long run. Even if you later delete something online, it lives on. My tweet was later published in the school paper and talked about quite a lot on campus. People were surprised that I'd lost my cool, and their image of me changed. I regret posting it. I could have talked with my teammates or called my parents. I didn't have to send my feelings out into cyberspace.

The day after I posted that tweet, after a restless night's sleep, I woke up and went to Saturday-morning practice. Things weren't normal, but we had a game on Sunday, and practice Saturday was vital.

Kelly Lindsey was there to greet us in the locker room. She'd joined our team as a volunteer assistant coach midway through the season—in fact, only two weeks before—but she was stepping in as our head coach. I was relieved. I liked Kelly, and I thought she could provide us with the leadership we needed.

We needed a pep talk, and she was ready to give it.

"I know yesterday was terrible," she said. "But you're a team. Your first few games were so strong, and that was because you played as a team. Just remember that teamwork is what's going to carry you through this. I'm looking around and seeing some smiles out there, and that's terrific. Your maturity through all of this is what's going to carry you through."

Our cocaptain, Brianna Bak, summed up our feelings pretty well when she talked to the school newspaper. "We're the ones that play anyway. A coach is a coach; players are what make a team." While she was more laid-back than I was (as if you couldn't tell from my tweet), I saw the truth in what she said. We had to hang together—it was all we had.

The following day, just two days after Neil quit, was our last non-conference game, and we played our hearts out. All we had were one another in our game against Santa Clara, ranked #11, and we worked as a team the entire time. Regulation ended in a tie, but after two fifteen-minute overtimes, it remained a draw.

We were disappointed, but I knew we'd be back. We'd start winning games, and we'd do it together, as a team.

Be Careful on Social Media

I'm incredibly active on social media now, and I always try to put my best foot forward. When you're going after your goals, the world needs to see that—and the world is watching you on social media. Even if you're feeling terrible, try to post something positive, like an inspirational quote (if you feel you have to post anything at all). People will see that you're trying to put something happy out into the world, and you'll get support for that. Remaining positive will also help you keep your head clear as you set goals and work toward them.

CHAPTER 16

We got the shock of our lives two days after the Santa Clara game. We were walking onto the field, ready to practice, and who was standing there but Neil. My jaw dropped.

What is he doing here? And what can he possibly have to say?

He called the team together, and believe it or not, he was apologetic.

"I'm so sorry I put all of you in this position. I had some personal issues I had to deal with last week, but I'm recommitting myself right here and now to this team. I love being a Cal Bear, and I want to do everything in my power to make this team win. Last week I put myself above our ideal of program, team, individual, and I'm sorry for that. It was wrong, and I owe each and every one of you an explanation and apology."

I was in disbelief. I'd been so upset at being abandoned so suddenly and under such mysterious circumstances. But now we had our coach back. Was I supposed to be happy? I just couldn't be. I was so angry with him, and I knew it would take a long time to fully accept his apology. We'd had a good relationship, and he'd helped me grow so much as a player. But that was in the past. He lost our trust the moment he walked out, and I wasn't ready to let my anger go. Nothing like this had ever happened to me before. Nobody had ever given up on me.

But I knew I had to think beyond myself. I was considered a leader on the team. I wasn't captain, but my commitment made people look to me for guidance.

I took a deep breath and cleared my mind, and I decided at that moment to do what Neil had suggested— put aside my own personal feelings for the good of the team. There was no way we could change the past, and Neil was here to stay. We had to stop thinking about our problems and move on.

And while I didn't realize it at the time, the drama with Neil was a good life lesson. We were adults now, and we had to learn that sometimes people let you down and sometimes they surpass your expectations. You never know; it's always a surprise. I'm not saying you shouldn't trust people, but you should be aware that sometimes they won't behave the way you expect. I think it's important to remember this, no matter your age.

In this case, I didn't have too much time to dwell, because the regular season began that very week. We had no choice but to move on with Neil as our coach. We had games to play, and we wanted to win them.

On Thursday morning, I took to Twitter, this time with a totally different tone than I'd had just days before.

Leaving for oregon. ready for the bears to kick some (butt)!

I had decided to think positive, and that had changed things for me. I was fired up and ready to start Pac-10 play. We were going to show the soccer world that we were united as a team, and we were going to win our first game against Oregon.

And we did.

Our 2–1 victory wasn't just a relief; it was exhilarating in many ways. We had just gone through something incredibly emotionally draining, but we hadn't let it defeat us. I'd also tied my college career high of nine goals in the season. At this rate, I was going to score at least sixteen that year, and that felt nothing short of amazing.

The rest of the season was up and down, but we held tight as a team. We had some amazing wins and some troubling losses, but I really felt like we'd tried our hardest. And finally, we'd found it in our hearts to forgive Neil. It had taken a few weeks. We'd even gone to Cal's athletic director and said that we didn't want to play with someone who'd given up on us.

"I understand your frustration, but he's not going anywhere," she said. "You have to deal with it."

So finally, we did. We started to trust him again, and things got better. Over the course of the season, Neil put in the effort to gain back our respect, and we learned to trust him, 100 percent. Eventually, what had felt like a major moment began to feel like just another bump in the road.

At 10-8-1 overall and 4-5-0 in the Pac-10, Cal earned an at-large bid in the NCAA tournament, meaning we hadn't won an automatic spot, but we'd been invited in by a panel of judges.

Our first game was against Auburn, and we won it fair and square in overtime. I scored the first goal; then Auburn came back to tie it up. We went into overtime, but Bears senior forward Lisa Kevorkian netted a beautiful shot at ninety-seven minutes, and the game was ours.

I was so happy for Lisa. Scoring a goal in overtime in the NCAA tournament was probably the biggest goal of her soccer career, and when she said her heart was "full to the point of bursting," I could tell. She was our hero for the day.

We were set to play #1-seeded Florida State in the second round, and we knew it was going to be a tough match. Florida State was one of the strongest teams in the nation, and for the seniors on our team, it was going to be a repeat of their freshman year, when they'd played FSU in the second round of the NCAA tournament. While we held them off till the thirty-fourth minute of play, they ended up scoring three goals in the second half, and they won it, ousting us from the tournament. It was a tough game, and they'd simply been better than us.

But I'd been so proud of our season, and getting to play in every game was an honor. No injuries and no national team commitments meant that I was with my team from start to finish, and I couldn't have been happier about that. My team was my family, and we'd been through so much that year that togetherness was everything to us.

Plus, there was always next year. . . .

Learn to Forgive

I'm very close with Neil and his family. Over the years he has helped me so much and been one of my biggest supporters. We talk and text all the time, I'm involved with the Cal team and community, and Neil was even recently a guest at my wedding! When you learn to forgive, accept that mistakes happen, and move forward, you can build an even stronger relationship, like the one I now have with Neil. People are human and make mistakes, and those errors can affect more people than intended, especially in team sports. But if you let them back in your life, your relationship can blossom in profound new ways, and they may even help you achieve your goals.

CHAPTER 17

I love Thanksgiving. I get to be with my family, eat great food, see old friends, and be thankful for all that life has given me. I've been so lucky, and I always reflect on that at Thanksgiving.

The phone rang Thanksgiving morning during my junior year, when I was still in my pajamas about to help Mom with the cooking. I didn't recognize the number on my phone, and besides, who calls on Thanksgiving? But I picked it up anyway.

"Alex, this is Cheryl Bailey," said a voice on the other end of the line. Cheryl was the general manager of the women's national team. Hearing her voice on the phone made my spine tingle.

She was brief. "We'd like you to come train with us. I hope you're healthy—you need to be prepared to play every day."

"Yes! Thank you! I'll be there!" I was practically breathless. "Thank you so much, Cheryl. I'm honored. I can't wait."

"Great, Alex," she replied. "I'm looking forward to meeting you."

When I hung up the phone, I had to contain my screams. This was it. This was the moment I'd been waiting for. Unless I really messed up at the camp, I'd soon be playing competition and friendly games with the national team, which might take me to the World Cup, the Olympics, and to a professional soccer career. I'd thought I'd probably get this call someday, but it had come much earlier than I'd expected. And on Thanksgiving morning, too!

I ran to tell my parents immediately, and the joy I could hear in their voices made my excitement level triple. I remembered all those days with Dad in the backyard, shooting goals. I remembered his patience and how he'd never put pressure on me, always letting me decide how seriously I wanted to pursue soccer. Mom had driven me to so many practices and so many games, and she'd never once complained. I was so thankful for them, and at that moment I felt like the luckiest girl in the world to have them as my parents. And to feel this kind of gratitude on Thanksgiving, too—it couldn't have been more fitting.

The US national training camp was going to start in December, so I had to get ready quickly. The camp was at the Home Depot Center in Carson, California, which was where I'd watched Mia Hamm, Joy Fawcett, and Julie Foudy's retirement game five years before. That game had been so personal to me—it was where I'd decided that I'd do everything in my power to become a professional soccer player—and going there felt like a homecoming to me. Plus, while I'd be staying in a hotel, I'd be close to my family, so I could see them every few days.

The team's head coach was Pia Sundhage. Remember her? She'd been sitting in the stands the previous year, watching me play the U-20 World Cup final. She'd replaced Coach Greg Ryan, who'd received a lot of criticism after a miserable loss for the team in the 2007 World Cup. Pia was a legend in her native Sweden—one of their national team's all-time best forwards—and she was very well liked in the United States. My idol Kristine Lilly had briefly played for her in Sweden and loved her so much that she said she wanted to play for her again.

Pia had a reputation as an easygoing and fun coach who also commanded respect. She was an authority figure, but a kind and sensible one. I liked that. Swedes have a reputation for being even-keeled and very professional, so it made sense to me that Pia would be a steady influence. But I realized I'd be standing in the company of giants with my other teammates, and *that* was intimidating. Forward Abby Wambach was one of the best players in the game, and Hope Solo was a goalkeeping legend. I was also going to be the youngest person there. Would they think I was a baby, or that I lacked the maturity to be there?

I was full of fear and had a million questions, but I couldn't let that hold me back. I remembered what happened when I went to the U-20 training camp, and I vowed that I wouldn't let nerves get the best of me. So I gathered my wits about me and got ready to go to training camp with the women's national team.

Camp was going to be ten days long. And believe it or not, it was smack-dab in the middle of finals. Thankfully, my professors were very understanding, and they worked with my schedule as far as year-end papers and tests went. Looking back on it, I think it was a good situation that I had so much to do then. When I got back to the hotel after days of training, I had to study immediately, and that took my mind off all the mistakes I'd made on the field. It also helped that there were a few other college-age girls there going through the same thing, so I didn't feel alone.

I'd been so nervous before going, but camp couldn't have been more productive or more fulfilling. We had one practice a day and played two friendly games, and we ate breakfast, lunch, and dinner together as a team, which gave us time to reflect on how we'd played.

Camp was also incredibly intense, both physically

and mentally. This was a whole different level of play. My teammates were just better than anyone I'd played with before. And everything felt like it was on a bigger scale—it was as if my field of vision grew as I became more technical and tactical. Pia was so positive, too. Everyone felt optimistic and excited to be out there. And while she was unlike Neil in a lot of ways, they're both European, so they brought a different style of play to the field.

Camp was only ten days, but I learned so much. When I completed my finals and went home to celebrate Christmas, I felt like I didn't even need any gifts because I'd already gotten the best one of all—a spot on the US Women's National Soccer Team.

Don't Let Fear Hold You Back

I was so nervous before going to camp. I'm always a little fearful before big events, but this was a whole new level. You'll probably be scared before a lot of the big tests you'll undertake while striving to reach your goals, but you can't let fear stand in your way. There's a saying that goes, "feelings aren't facts," and this is true. Just because you're scared doesn't mean there is *actually* something to fear. So be bold and dive into the challenge. It's okay to be nervous, but don't let it hold you back—you can do it!

CHAPTER 18

After camp was over I quickly got word that *another* national team training camp was going to be held at the Home Depot Center at the end of January and beginning of February. Twenty-six players were called up, and the purpose was to let Pia get one more look at the team to decide which nineteen players would be selected to attend the Algarve Cup. The Algarve Cup is one of the oldest and most important soccer tournaments of the international scene, and it's held every year in Portugal. It one of three championships in women's soccer, along with the Olympics and the World Cup. It's not as prestigious as those, but it's still a big deal.

My nerves had quieted down a little bit because I'd gotten to know the rest of the team at the last camp, but this time something big was on the line—play at my first senior international tournament. I realized that I was somewhat of a long shot, given that I was so young and so new, but I wanted so badly to be one of the players chosen.

The United States had lost to Sweden in last year's Algarve Cup—on penalty kicks, no less—so this was going to be a heated year with the States hunting for the win. Despite being the winningest team in the Cup's history, we felt like we had a lot to prove. Plus, the United States was set to play Sweden in the group stage at this year's tournament, which meant Pia was going to go against her own country again. Needless to say, it was going to be an interesting game!

I'm getting ahead of myself. I was so excited about the camp, but it fell right at the beginning of the semester. I was the only college player called to this extended camp, which was a big honor, but also *very* intimidating. I'd miss three weeks of classes and have to study back at the hotel, and I was worried I'd have to drop a class. Either that or I'd fall so far behind I'd never catch up. Do you ever have those dreams where you realize, weeks into school, that you haven't attended any of the classes and that you have a test coming up? Well, that was actually happening to me—and I wasn't dreaming!

I was also concerned that my studies might interfere with my performance on the field. If I couldn't stay completely focused on soccer—if I was preoccupied with studying and school during practice or at team meetings—would that affect my contributions to the team? I made a vow right then and there that I had to divide and balance my time better than I ever had before. If I was on the field, my life would be soccer. Off the field, school. I'd always done this. Why should now be any different?

The first few days of camp were wonderful. I was so excited to see my teammates, who at that point were starting to feel like old friends. At the last camp I'd struck up an immediate friendship with my roommate, Heather O'Reilly, who was just a little bit older than me but had been on the national team for years. She knew Neil, so we connected about that, and in general, she was just so sweet to me. Abby Wambach had been similarly welcoming. She'd told me to come to her for anything, and she was always checking in with me. Finally, Amy Rodriguez and I would go get coffee every morning and hang out. We were both known for our speed, and as forwards we had tons to talk about.

I was pretty upbeat about whatever my future might hold. If I didn't get selected for the Algarve Cup team, I'd still have my senior year at Cal ahead of me. I wouldn't be playing with the national team, but maybe the phone would ring again, with Cheryl on the other end, calling me up to a training camp. Just because you don't get selected for one tournament doesn't mean you're out of the running forever. And like I said, I'd still have Cal and my beloved varsity team, which had taught me so much. Either way, I'd be training every day, playing the sport that made my heart sing.

I was truly lucky to have so many options. But no matter what happened, I wanted to feel like I'd tried my hardest and played my best. If I didn't get picked for the Algarve Cup, it wouldn't be a failure. There was always next time. I felt as confident as I could be, but then the unexpected happened.

On the third day of practice, I was running down the field and felt an uncomfortable pain in the back of my leg. I thought, *Maybe it's just a strain?* So I kept running.

But after a few more steps I skidded to a halt and bent down, trying to stretch the back of my legs. It hurt worse than before. I shook my leg. *Maybe it's just tight?* But when it still didn't feel better, I knew immediately—I had a hamstring injury.

Most of you probably know what your hamstring is, but if you don't, I'll tell you. It's the long muscle in the back of your leg that you can feel if you bend down and touch your toes. Runners often strain their hamstrings because they put a lot of pressure on them as they're sprinting. It's so important to stretch because that can ease a lot of the tension that builds up in your hamstrings. I'd been stretching—a lot—but obviously, I'd been running a lot too. And maybe it had been just too much for my body to handle.

I went to the sidelines and talked to the team trainers. They examined my leg and confirmed I had hurt my hamstring. This wasn't a major injury, and I knew it was possible I'd recover quickly, so I took stock of the situation.

I was pretty bummed, but I was sure of one thing: I didn't want to sit out a practice. And I wasn't ready to go home. So I asked them if they thought I would be able to continue playing. The trainers said they'd wrap my leg tight first for compression and see how I felt.

Awesome, I thought. This was promising.

With my leg wrapped up, I jumped back into practice and started sprinting. But I felt immediate pain, and right away I knew I'd strained it even more. Unfortunately, it was going to be a few weeks until I was back on the field.

At age twenty, I was not just the youngest player at the national team training camp, but I was the first to leave. I was brokenhearted. This was my first shot at a senior international tournament, and I wasn't going to make it. But I knew it wasn't my fault—*everyone* gets hurt in soccer at one time or another—and as far as injuries go, pulling a hamstring wasn't bad. I knew I could recover. This wasn't going to end my career, and it was a fraction as bad as tearing my ACL. Also, I had the experience of having been through something like this once before, and I'd come out on top. I knew I'd be back and better than ever.

Make a Plan B

You may have your heart set on something, but if you don't achieve it or don't get selected for it, you have to turn to your plan B. Cal was my plan B, and when I pulled my hamstring and had to leave the national training camp, I wasn't just resigned to going back—I was delighted. My plan B was a good one. I think you always have to have something in your back pocket, and you have to be sure that it's something you'll be happy with. Maybe you didn't get into Harvard. That's okay—you still got into a backup school you'll love. So many things in life are out of your control, but you *can* control your destiny if you have a few possibilities to fall back on.

CHAPTER 19

The Algarve Cup wasn't on television, but I checked in on the results every few days. And in between, I focused on my studies and getting myself healthy. There were nineteen members of the US national team fighting their hearts out in Portugal, and while I wasn't with them, I was there in spirit. I'll never know whether or not I would have been selected for the team, and maybe that is for the best. The time between my injury and the start of the Cup had given me the space to feel nothing but excitement for my friends. Amy, Shannon, Abby, and all the wonderful women I'd come to love played absolutely beautifully over the course of the tournament, and after a hard-fought final against Germany, the United States prevailed 3–2.

My recovery from my hamstring injury was quick—so fast, in fact, that I was feeling ready to play by the beginning of March. Being sidelined is tough. I missed playing so much. But like my previous injury, the break gave me time and space to rediscover my passion for the sport.

I was getting anxious to show everyone I was 100 percent again when the phone rang. It was Cheryl Bailey.

"Alex," said Cheryl's voice on the end of the line. "We'd like you to play in a friendly game against Mexico at the end of the month. The match is in Utah, so we'll need you a few days early for training."

I grinned from ear to ear. I would have packed my bags right then if she'd asked. But this was only a few weeks away, so I didn't have long to wait.

When we arrived in Sandy, Utah, which is a suburb of Salt Lake City, the forecast called for snow. As you know, I'm from Southern California, so I had zero experience playing in snow. Pia probably played one hundred games in snow in Sweden, and Abby Wambach's from Rochester, New York, so I'm sure it's no big deal for her. But for me? I couldn't even imagine it. I thought of the players from Mexico—had they ever even *seen* snow? This was going to be crazy!

Sure enough, it started coming down before the game and didn't stop the whole time. I walked toward the field feeling like a kid on a snow day—a very cold and wet kid, mind you. I couldn't wait to play.

But there were two things that made the day even more exciting.

First, Pia had told me before the game that she wanted to put me in for about forty-five minutes. I wasn't tapped to start, but she wanted to see me on the field, and she expected it would be for the entire second half. *I can't believe it*, I thought. *My first international game with the US national women's team. I'm only twenty years old, and my dream is really coming true.*

But even better, my idol Kristine Lilly was playing with the national team for the first time since 2007. She'd taken a few years off from the team, but she'd decided she wanted to come back, and Pia had called her up for this game. She had worn #13 long before I did—I felt like she *owned* it—so that's the jersey she wore, and I wore #21.

One day I told Kristine I'd always worn #13 in her honor.

"Well, Alex," she replied. "When I retire, number thirteen is yours."

I was so honored, and to this day Kristine's words mean so much to me. Every time I put on my #13 jersey, I think of what an amazing player she was, and I still strive to be as successful as she was.

But that day, as we stood waiting for the game to begin, Abby turned to the rest of the team and said, "If we score, we're doing snow angels. And if we go two up, it's snowball-fight time."

We all laughed. Abby is our spiritual leader in many ways. She makes us laugh all the time, has such a big heart, and thinks of the good of the team before she thinks of herself. She's tough but completely loving. Anyway, three inches of snow? It was going to make for terrible playing conditions, but Abby wanted us to see the fun in it. It hadn't ever snowed during a US women's national game, so why not turn it into something memorable?

And it was. We were sliding all over the place, snow pelting our bare legs and blinding our eyes, and sometimes you'd try to make a pass and the ball would roll and then get stuck. We even had to play with a bright yellow ball so the players could see it! We were scoreless in the first half, and I took to the field in the forty-sixth minute. *My first senior national game.* I was so happy.

Then Abby scored in the sixtieth minute off a one-yard tap into the goal, and she headed straight for the right corner of the field, where she lay down and started making snow angels. And then everyone else joined in! Even a few midfielders who weren't near the goal dropped to the ground and made their own. There I was near Abby, freezing to death in three inches of powder, making a snow angel, and I thought I'd died and gone to heaven. Who knew hard work could be so fun?

We won against Mexico 1–0, so there was no snowball fight, but all in all, it was a day to remember. Never again has it snowed on a US women's national game, and we certainly made the most of it!

Treat Yourself

When you reach a goal, don't forget to celebrate. I'll never forget that day playing Mexico, mainly because it was my first senior national game, and of course, because of the snow angels. I think we all get caught up in the relentless push toward a goal, and sometimes when we make it, we're so tired that we don't stop to appreciate the accomplishment. But being happy and throwing a little party for yourself shows that you deserve what you've achieved. Treat yourself well and have fun!

CHAPTER 20

The friendly matches the United States was playing during the spring of 2010 were in many ways preparation for the World Cup, which was going to be held in Germany the following summer. You might think that a year is a long time to get ready for something, but it's really not. If you're going to take something seriously and do your best, you have to think *far* ahead. We were already thinking about the summer of 2011, and we hadn't even qualified for the World Cup yet. That would take place later that year (we hoped!)

So as I headed into the spring and summer of 2010, I realized I had some hard decisions to make. If I was going to put my all into the women's national team, I had to shift my emphasis away from school. There was also just no way I could be absent from school in my last semester, training with the team, and still graduate on time.

In addition, the WPS—the Women's Professional Soccer league—would be holding its draft in the coming months, and I was pretty sure I was going to be picked for a team. That meant I'd be playing professional soccer—actually making money doing the thing I loved the most—in addition to playing with the national team. It was time for me to move on from college, as much as I knew I'd miss it. But I'd gone to Cal with a dream, and that was to play soccer full-time. In order to accomplish your goals, you have to make tough choices, and that time had come for me.

I decided I was going to graduate early. You may be thinking, *How is that possible?* But I realized if I took classes during the summer, I could finish up my degree by the end of the fall semester. I had two semesters left, so why not take one during the summer? I'd have to be absent occasionally to train with the national team, but that was nothing new—I'd done that the previous fall. *I can do this*, I told myself.

A lot of high-level collegiate athletes—including several members of the women's national team—have left college to pursue professional sports full-time. That's a personal decision, and I don't think it's something that can be taken lightly. But it wasn't for me. My parents had always stressed the importance of a degree, so it was something I valued. And I was *so* close to graduating that leaving without my diploma felt silly. I knew that if I just stepped up my game, I could graduate early!

But first I had to join the national team in a friendly

game against Germany, which was going to be held on May 22 in Cleveland. I doubted I'd get a chance to start—I was still so new to the team—but I at least wanted a chance to make a mark with them. If I could get a goal, I'd be in heaven. All in all, I just wanted to contribute to my team.

Germany is an absolute powerhouse in soccer, on both the men's side and the women's side. If you watched the men's World Cup in 2014, you'll remember them beating Argentina decisively. The German women's team was consistently ranked by FIFA judges as one of the best in the world, but we were always considered to be just a bit better.

More than ten thousand people were in attendance that day—it was a *huge* crowd. And after a hard-fought game, we won 4–0! I got to play starting midway through the second half, and while I didn't score, I was pleased with my progress.

I was starting to feel at home with the national team. It was still a little surreal playing with Abby and Shannon Boxx and especially Kristine Lilly, but it was beginning to get a little easier. I was still the new kid, but I was proving myself. And I kept getting called up for games, which showed I was making progress.

That summer, I worked like crazy. I took a full load of classes, played a few friendly games with the women's national team, and practiced soccer every single day. I had a goal in my sights, and that was to graduate early and move on to a professional career. It was a stressful summer, but I loved multitasking, and most of all, I loved working toward something.

I even practiced with the Cal men's team! It was so much fun being on the field with Servando. He was also gearing up for his last semester, and he was hoping to be drafted by a professional team in early 2011. I knew he would be—he was an excellent player and was cocaptain of the Cal men's team our senior year.

I wondered what the future would hold for us. It was likely he'd go play in one city and I'd play in another. Plus, I'd be traveling all the time with the national team. Being apart for short periods of time was nothing new for us—we'd done it all through college—but living in different cities? That really scared me. I realized then I'd just have to trust in what we had. He was my best friend as well as one of the most passionate soccer players I knew. If that didn't hold us together, I didn't know what would.

Let Go

When you're working toward something, you often have to trust in the unknown. I know that's hard. When you strive for something every day, you just want to be in control of everything! But you can't be. There are invisible forces in the world that are beyond your reach, and you just have to trust in them. It was my goal to play soccer full-time, and it was Servando's, too. What that would mean for our relationship was largely out of our control, but we had to have faith in each other and in the world. If we were meant to be together, we would be. Letting go and having faith things will work out for the best is tough, but it's all you can do sometimes.

CHAPTER 21

As I stood on the field before the first Bears game of my senior year, things felt a little bittersweet. On the one hand, I was moving on to what I'd always dreamed of—the women's professional draft and the national team—but I was leaving behind so much. I was going to graduate in December, leave my beloved college team behind, and say good-bye to dear friends I'd known for four years, not to mention being away from my boyfriend for long stretches of time. Cal had taught me so much on the field and off. It had taken me to Italy and Spain and Switzerland, introduced me to some of the finest teachers in the world, and brought my soccer game to a whole new level. In many ways, I had grown up here, and I was truly sad to leave.

Each time you move on to a new step in life, you'll be forced to say good-bye to people and places you love. As you set goals, you also have to come to grips with the fact that you may have to leave a lot behind you on your way to attaining them. Just remember that the people and places you love are always a part of you because they've helped make you who you are.

I knew I wouldn't be playing many games with the Bears that season. With the World Cup qualifying tournament looming, I'd be training with the national team for long stretches. So I resolved to make the most of every single game. I really wanted to appreciate these final games as much as I possibly could.

And that sense of gratitude I was feeling was amplified even more when I got a few early-season honors. I was named to the Hermann Trophy short list again, and I was chosen as a Lowe's Senior CLASS Award candidate, a prize awarded to students who'd excelled in community, classroom, character, and competition. I'd always liked multitasking, so this nomination was a real honor. During a few early-season games in which I played my heart out, I scored a hat trick in one game and scored five goals in one weekend. We were unbeaten by mid-September, with a record of five wins, no losses, and three ties. What a great start! I felt like I was giving it my all, which was exactly what I'd wanted to do. I wanted to go out giving this team everything I could.

Neil had also implemented a motto for the team this year: "Live Like Champions." I loved it—I think feeling like a champion *in your heart and soul* will make you radiate progress and purpose. Being a champion isn't just about winning, though. It's about putting your best foot forward on the field and off. To "live like champions" Neil had laid out a twelve-point plan that would make us accomplish three objectives: have the highest GPAs of any team on campus, be the best players possible on the field, and give back to the community. We dove into the plan headfirst, doing training camps for younger athletes, volunteering in the community, and working harder than we ever had on the field and in the classroom. We had solid, tangible goals, and I think it made us all happier. I know I was happier.

With my heart full and a sense of real purpose from my time spent with the Bears, I was called up for training with the national team barely a month into my senior year. There were two friendly games with China coming up—one in Kennesaw, Georgia, and one in Philadelphia—and Pia had set up a training camp outside of Atlanta for thirty of us. This was going to be an interesting camp. Most of the players on the squad were on WPS teams, and many of them were in the midst of playoffs. So it would be a smaller group of us at first—basically, everyone who wasn't in a playoff—and then, as teams were eliminated before the WPS championship on September 26, other players would come down.

These early games against China were important for both the players and the coaches. First and foremost, they were essentially warm-ups before the World Cup qualifying tournament, which was going to be held in Cancún, Mexico, from October 28 to November 9. The camp and these games gave us a chance to bond again and work on tactical elements. It had been months since I'd played with the team, and I knew I needed some quality time with my friends to feel at home on the field with them. For Pia and the assistant coaches, this was a chance to look at who would be on the roster for the final qualifying tournament team. So this camp and the games against China were like tryouts for me—I was by no means a shoo-in for the World Cup qualifying team, and I really needed to prove myself.

This time, I wasn't the only collegiate player at the camp. Remember Sydney Leroux, whom I'd played with in the U-20 World Cup? She was there! This was her first call-up to the national team, and like me, it had happened when she was a junior. I was so excited to see her there—she and I had become so close during the World Cup—and I couldn't wait to catch up on all that had happened in the almost two years since we'd played together.

I felt so much more at home with the team this time around. It was my third training camp with them, and they felt like old friends. I knew we had some tough matches ahead of us, but I felt confident. Living like a champion at Cal the past month had improved my outlook immensely. This was my big opportunity. The World Cup loomed in the not-too-distant future, and I was determined to get there.

Give Back

Neil's "Live Like Champions" philosophy and plan was a wonderful way to help me reach my goals. But I think the most important thing it taught me was that when you set your goals and go after them, they can't be all about you. You have to give back. I loved coaching younger players and volunteering in the community—the positive energy I felt from helping others stayed with me and followed me onto the field. So when you're pursuing your dreams, don't be selfish. Find ways to help others. I promise the good vibes you get from it will make your entire life better.

CHAPTER 22

The United States and China have always had a big soccer rivalry, going back to 1986. We'd gone against them forty-two times since 1986, which was more than we'd played practically any team. We'd won most of those games, but they were still fierce competitors. We hadn't lost to anyone on US soil in six years, though, so the pressure was on to really perform.

I hadn't been chosen for the team roster for the first game, but I had for the second. I was disappointed about the first game, but it was okay. I was still very much the new kid on the team, and I realized that I could learn a lot just by watching them play. Plus, I'd have my chance a few days later in the second game.

The United States won the first exhibition game 2–1 against China. The score should have been higher. We outshot China 20–6 and dominated the field, but we struggled with finishing and, in general, weren't attacking like we should. But the purpose of these games was to learn something, and that's what we were going to do. Megan Rapinoe, a really crafty midfielder with long, powerful kicks, had led the game with five terrific shots, one of which went in. Games like this allow certain players to show their stuff, and that's what Megan got to do. I hoped I'd have my chance soon.

I wasn't going to be a starter in the second game, but I would be a sub. Pia had determined that I was a good mid-to-late-game threat, so she was going to put me in for the second half to change the dynamics of the game. I liked my reputation as someone who could come in late and really shake things up, but deep down I wanted the world to see that I could not only make it a whole game, but be consistently strong from start to finish. I'd done that at Cal and on the U-20 team, so I knew I could do it here.

But so much of soccer is about being strategic, and that's what Pia was trying to do. She thought I could change the energy on the field. I was fast, and when people are starting to feel worn down in the second half, it's often smart to get a fresh set of legs out there.

We were playing in Chester, Pennsylvania, outside of Philadelphia, at PPL Park, where the Philadelphia Union play. My parents were up there in the stands cheering me on. This was only my third international game with the senior team, but something about this felt bigger. Maybe it was the World Cup qualifying tournament looming, or maybe I had a sixth sense about something. All I knew was that I was living like a champion, and I felt great.

I watched from the sidelines as the United States started off strong, but crumbled in the thirty-seventh minute when a beautiful pass from one Chinese player to another resulted in a twelve-yard volley into the goal. There was nothing we could have done once her foot hit the ball—it was just a great shot, perfectly executed.

Halftime came and went, and I began to get itchy about going in. I was warmed up, and I was ready. Pia's plan was for me and Yael Averbuch to come in as subs at the same time—sort of a double threat against the Chinese at a time when they were feeling vulnerable. She was going to change the formation at the same time to further confuse them. It seemed like a great plan.

In the seventy-first minute, I got my chance. Yael and I ran onto the field, and immediately the energy changed. We started to really put the pressure on, attacking in a way we hadn't in the first half. But what was so interesting to me was the way I started connecting with Abby Wambach.

I've talked a little bit about Abby, but I can't say enough about what a positive force on the field she is. She is our top scorer, has an uncanny ability to get shots in off her head, and is pure power and technical skill. She is the player we pass to in the hopes of getting goals.

Over the course of the last few practices, Abby and I had developed a really good dynamic. My speed and her powerful energy were a winning combination.

In the eighty-third minute, we put that teamwork into practice. Yael initially got the ball and tapped it over to Heather Mitts. Heather kicked it—hard—and sent it over the heads of the Chinese line, where it met Abby, who was sprinting down the field toward the goal. It landed in front of her, bounced high, and connected with her forehead. She knocked it right into my path. I dribbled it a few more yards down the field and then shot with my left foot.

Now, I have two things I tell myself when I make a shot. One, I *always* use my left foot when I can. It's my strong foot, and I'm more precise with it. It's also a little more unusual to be left-footed, so it throws people off. And two, never look the goalkeeper in the eyes. You don't want her to know where you're shooting.

I did both of those, and the ball cut through the air perfectly toward the goal, where it went right into the left side.

GOOOOAAALLLLLL!!!!

I'd scored my first international goal with the senior national team. I was twenty-one years old, the only college player on the team, and I'd tied up the game. There were so many things running through my head at that moment that I couldn't tell you exactly what I was thinking, but I know I was the happiest I've been in my life. I ran toward my teammates, and the first person who hugged me was Kristine Lilly, my childhood idol and now my teammate. I can't think of anything more fitting or more meaningful. It was an honor just to be on the field with her, but for her to congratulate me? It meant everything.

We didn't score the rest of the game, but tying 1–1 saved us from losing on US soil—something we hadn't done for six years. And Pia later said that we learned some important lessons during the game, and in the end, that's what matters. Changing things around in the second half really saved us, and the goal assist with Abby began to cement a bond I still have with her. I was thrilled.

Master the Basics

Goal setting often requires you to master a few fundamentals—the things you *always* do because you know you can do them well, or because they are part of a foolproof plan. My mantras are (1) know your strengths—for me, it's allowing my left foot to be my dominant foot—and (2) never look goalkeepers in the eye. Yours might include always running three steps between the hurdles on the one-hundred-yard hurdle sprint; filling in the bubbles on a standardized test only after you've completed all the questions; or making sure your posture is correct when you're playing the guitar. I'm not saying you're going to fail if you don't follow your fundamentals—sometimes you have to shake things up or accommodate a change. But it's good to master some basics. If you have them down, you can always fall back on them.

CHAPTER 23

I wasn't guaranteed a place on the World Cup qualifying team. Pia had to narrow down the thirty players who'd been at camp to twenty who'd be playing at the tournament in Mexico, which was going to be held at the end of October and beginning of November. I was feeling slightly more confident after making a goal in the game against China, but by no means did I think I was home free.

Plus, I knew choosing the final roster was going to be tough for Pia and the other coaches. There wasn't a single player who'd been at the camp who wasn't qualified, but decisions had to be made. I just hoped I was good enough.

Breathe, I told myself. *Just breathe and be patient.*

I'm sure you've waited for news to come, whether it's the cast list for the school play or an acceptance letter to college. It's so nerve-racking, but you just have to be patient. Try as hard as possible not to lose sleep or go crazy with worry—the news will come when it's going to come, and it's often out of your control. Like I told myself at the time, just remember to breathe!

The whole team heard the news of who'd made the cut while we were gathered together at the end of camp. Pia stood in front of us with a big paper-covered easel behind her.

"You've all worked so hard this camp. I'm so proud of you—all of you. Even the players going home. I can only choose twenty people, but please know that you've all played beautifully."

She turned back to the easel and flipped over a piece of paper. I scanned the list of names, and there was my name. *I'd done it.*

I was so excited, but I contained myself. Some of my teammates were going home, so celebrating just wasn't appropriate.

But inside, words can't describe how happy I felt. From the first time I watched the World Cup in 1999, I had dreamed about this day. Every single practice had been played with one major goal in mind, and that was a chance to play in the World Cup.

When I got back to my room I called my parents and started gushing.

"Mom, Dad, I'm on the World Cup qualifying team. We're going to Mexico to play at the end of the month." My voice was shaking.

My mom was crying. "Alex, I am so proud of you. This is what you've been working for, and you did it. You did it!"

I knew they'd always been proud of me, but this was at a whole different level. I thanked them for everything they'd ever done for me—all those hours of practice, all that money they'd poured into teams and coaches and driving me around. It had all paid off. While I wasn't guaranteed to play in the World Cup—we had to qualify, and I had to be chosen for the final team—I was still going to Mexico to play for our team's spot.

Pia had pulled together a great squad. Ten of the players had gone to the Olympics in 2008, and seven had been to the World Cup. Kristine Lilly had been to four World Cups, and Abby Wambach had been to two. But for more than half of us, this would be a completely new experience, and as Pia said, the team was a mixture of veterans, who brought experience, and new players, who would add inspiration. I hoped I lived up to the task.

Before I left for Mexico, I played my last official Bears home game. It wasn't the last game for the other seniors, but since I had to travel to Mexico, it was the final one for me. I was pretty sure I could hold it together—after all, I'd known for a long time that this was coming—but right when I stepped onto the field, I got pretty emotional, which was unusual for me. We won against Washington State that day, and all the seniors were honored with flowers and a really sweet send-off. Then we had a barbeque after the game with our families and the rest of the team. I'd be back for the NCAA tournament, but boy, I was going to miss the team in the meantime. They had meant so much to me.

But wonderful things lay ahead in my future, and I had to remember that.

It's Not Over Till It's Over

Just after I left for Cancún to train with the national team, I did an interview for the Cal newspaper. The interviewer asked me what was the most important thing I learned at Cal, and it didn't take me long to think of an answer. I said that you should always work hard, never give up, and fight until the end because it's never really over until the whistle blows. And that holds true no matter what your goal—if it's getting into a college, making a varsity team, or getting cast in the school play. There is no reason you should give up before you know the outcome. Your fight isn't over until time is called.

CHAPTER 24

The CONCACAF World Cup qualifying tournament worked a little differently than most tournaments, so bear with me while I explain it. CONCACAF stands for "The Confederation of North, Central American, and Caribbean Association Football," and it is the governing body for soccer in all of those areas. Other continents have their own confederations. Not every country in the world can go to the World Cup (you'd have hundreds of teams there if that were the case!), so you have to hold tournaments to narrow it all down. In the case of CONCACAF, there were eight teams fighting for two guaranteed spots.

There were two groups of teams—group A and group B. We'd play three games within each group, and the top two finishers from each group would go to the semifinals. So there would be four teams in the semis. If you won in the semifinals, you went to the finals and were automatically in the World Cup. If you lost in the semis, you played the other group's loser in the semis. If you won that, you were given third place, but you'd have to play a European team to decide if you'd go to the Cup. Confused? I'll simplify it. The only way to guarantee entry into the World Cup was to win first or second place at the CONCACAF tournament. Third place was still iffy, and you'd have to play a European team to make it in.

We were ranked #1 in the world, and CONCACAF had never given us much competition—in fact, it had always been a blowout—so we were feeling confident going in. On the other hand, we'd come in third place in the 2007 World Cup, which had been a disappointment, so we felt we had something to prove. We weren't going to take the World Cup lightly. If anything, we were determined to dominate. But I'm getting ahead of myself—first we had to *get into* the World Cup tournament, which meant winning CONCACAF.

Our first game was against Haiti, and it was heartbreaking on many levels. You probably remember the 2010 earthquake in Haiti, which killed hundreds of thousands of people and threw the country into complete chaos, poverty, and despair. The headquarters of the Haitian Football Federation had collapsed during the earthquake, killing thirty-two members, including the women's team coach. Now, the game was only ten months later, so we were shocked that Haiti was even there. Their team was funded by donations, and I have no idea where they'd found the space to practice as they'd fought to pull their lives back together. And they'd lost their *coach*. I can't even begin to imagine their pain.

I am a firm believer in giving back, and the needs of the Haitians were so great. So we'd all decided that when the game was over, we were going to give the Haitian team cleats, clothes, gear, and other game-related items we'd brought along with us. We had too much, and they had next to nothing—it was the least we could do. As I've said before, you always have to think about others, especially in times of need.

Our hearts were with them as we played—and they played so well. But we were just too powerful for them, and we won 5–0. Abby scored a hat trick—the fifth of her senior national career—and Rachel Buehler netted her first international goal. Even though they'd lost, this was the best Haiti had ever played against us, and we were aware of how hard they'd fought. After the game, we told them.

"Please accept these gifts from us; I hope they help out your team and families," Abby said as we met them in their locker room after the game. "We've been thinking of you, and we wish you all the best in the rest of the tournament. We loved playing with you today."

We posed for photos and hugged, and I felt a real

kinship with them. Soccer has an amazing way of bringing people together, even if you're opponents.

Two days later, we beat Guatemala 9–0. Amy Rodriguez scored a hat trick, Megan Rapinoe and Abby each made two goals, and I scored at the beginning of the second half. My second international goal! We were starting to feel *very* confident—fourteen goals in two days of play? Not bad at all.

Our third and final game in the group stage was just as decisive. We were playing Costa Rica, and we beat them 4–0. I netted the final goal of the game eighty-one minutes in. Hooray! We had shut out every team we played in the group stage, sending us into the semifinals full of confidence. We were going to the World Cup—we were sure of it. Only Mexico stood in our way.

Make Charity Personal

I talked earlier about giving back to the community and how the positive energy you get from it will help you in all areas of your life, specifically as you try to reach your goals. But let me be a little more specific. Making a personal connection to someone you help is even more important. It's one thing to give money to a charity—and believe me, I'm not downplaying that at all. Charities need your money and your donations. But it's another to give your time, so do that too! Speaking with the Haitian team showed us firsthand what they were going through, and it motivated us more to be there for them and others in need. So I encourage you to tutor, volunteer in a soup kitchen, or even just *speak* to someone you're helping. Make charity personal.

CHAPTER 25

W e had four days of rest; then we were set to play Mexico in the semifinals. Mexico was a good team, but we'd beaten them every single time we'd played them. All twenty-six appearances. Not a single loss. On the other hand, they were the home team, so the fans would be cheering against us (except for my parents, who were up there rooting for me, as always!). But skill, history, and our dominant record in the tournament were on our side, and we felt fairly confident we'd move on to the finals. After all, we were one of the best teams in the world.

There was a capacity crowd of 8,500 people that night in Cancún, and the weather was remarkably cool at sixty degrees. But we'd be running so much we'd warm up fast. It wasn't like we were playing in snow, like we had in our last match with Mexico!

I wasn't slated to start, which didn't come as a surprise. This was a big game for us, and we needed veterans on the field, especially at the start of the game. As you know, my special skill had been coming into the second half as a substitute, changing the energy of the team when our opponents were getting a little tired.

Even though we'd shut out other qualifying opponents handily, we'd struggled a little during the first halves of those games. There had been something missing—we just weren't playing as well as we should have been. And Pia wanted us to work on that during that day's game against Mexico.

The energy in the stands was noticeable when we entered the stadium—the fans were rowdy, loud, and were definitely *not* rooting for us. We were playing in a baseball stadium, so fans were a lot closer to us than they usually are. They even threw beer cans and trash on the field! Sometimes crowds are referred to as "the twelfth player" because they play such a big role in the dynamics of the game, and I knew right away this would put us at a disadvantage.

The whistle blew, and things were off to a bad start almost immediately. Two minutes in, one of Mexico's best players, Maribel Domínguez, ran under a pass from one of her teammates and sprinted toward our goal with her eyes on the ball, which landed just ahead of her. She was so fast we couldn't even defend her, and when she made it to the ball, she tapped it right past our goalkeeper. There was no way to save it. We'd been caught off guard, and only three minutes in, we were down 1–0.

I can't begin to describe to you how stunned we were. It felt like we'd been kicked in the gut—three minutes of play, and we were already losing? We hadn't even had a chance to warm up, and already we were down.

We had to start fighting. From the sidelines I could tell our play looked lackluster, and the energy of the crowd was hurting us. But slowly . . . slowly . . . our momentum began to build. We were going to come back.

And sure enough, in the twenty-fifth minute of play, we got our chance. Megan Rapinoe took the corner kick. She is so strong and so precise on long kicks, and she's become our go-to person for corners and penalty kicks—so we knew at that moment she could be a threat. The ball flew long and landed right in the middle of the penalty area into a mass of players. The Mexican goalkeeper attempted to clear it, but she didn't get it far. The ball landed right in front of Carli Lloyd, and she slid to the ground with her legs extended out in front of her. Just as she landed, she kicked the ball into the right side of the goal.

We had tied! There was a palpable sense of relief on the field, but we knew our job wasn't done. Games don't end in a tie during the semifinal stage of a tournament like this. Instead, you play through overtime and penalty kicks till someone wins.

I could sense us getting our confidence back. But just two minutes after Carli's goal, our hopes were dashed again. A Mexican player named Verónica Pérez caught a cross from the right side and headed the ball beautifully into the left side of the goal. It was the kind of shot Abby always got—fast and hard and diving into the goal. The Mexican fans went wild.

A little more than twenty minutes later we went into the locker room for halftime with our hearts in our stomachs. How could we be down 2–1 to a team we'd always beaten? The United States had never—not once—failed to make it to the finals of the World Cup qualifying tournament, and now here we were, losing. There was still the second half ahead of us—a half I'd get to play in—but it was going to be an uphill battle we hadn't expected.

In the end, we didn't win the game against Mexico. They beat us 2–1. We took some shots on goal that could have gone in, but the Mexican defense was too strong, and our finishing just wasn't good. Everyone has theories of why we didn't win—the backfield was weak; Abby had to leave the game for a few minutes because she had a collision with another player and was bleeding from her head; our shots just weren't precise. All of those things are correct, but the lesson we all learned was that "the greatest upset in women's soccer history" (as the press called it) happened because the Mexican team played better than they've ever played. And that's what you *always* have to do, on the field and off. Play hard and fight like crazy till a job is done.

I'd thought we were invincible, but we weren't.

Don't Make Excuses

When we lost to Mexico, we could have blamed it on the crowd or Abby's unexpected injury. Taking too much time to find blame and make excuses for why you didn't win takes you away from focusing on the future. The thousand reasons why things didn't go right are in the past, and saying "it's not my fault" is just a waste of time. Take stock, learn something from the mistakes you made, and move ahead.

CHAPTER 26

Abby said something so true in an interview at the end of the CONCACAF World Cup qualifying tournament. She commented that any team—even the #1 team in the world (which was us)—will lose. Soccer's just one of those games where everyone loses at one point or another. But she added, "It's a wake-up call for everyone, and we're going to work our tails off to make sure it never happens again."

When you're going after your goals, you have to accept that you're going to lose sometimes. It's part of life. But you can learn from it and work harder because of it. And that was our plan for the next three games.

Yes, we had to play three games to get into the World Cup. One game would be against Costa Rica, who had lost to Canada in the semifinal. If we won that, we'd have two games against Italy, who had placed #5 in the European Cup. We'd play one game in Italy and one game at home, and whoever had the most goals at the end would go to the World Cup.

You'll remember that we'd played Costa Rica earlier in the group stage of the tournament and had beaten them 4–0. So we were feeling confident going into this game. Then again, we'd been confident going into the game against Mexico, so we made sure to be ready for anything this time.

We played our hearts out and beat Costa Rica 3–0. *Whew.* It was such a relief. But we knew our work wasn't over—two more games still stood between us and the World Cup. We were ready to take on Italy.

The weekend before the national team left for Italy for the first of our two games against them, I reunited with my Cal teammates for the first game in the NCAA tournament. We had finished up our season 15-2-0 and 7-2-0 in the Pac-10, and we were set to play Duke. Initially, Pia had forbidden me from going—she didn't want me to risk injury before a big game. But I begged her, and finally she and I agreed that I could attend the tournament as long as I didn't play. I just wanted one more chance to be with the Cal team—they were so important to me, and even if I couldn't play, I needed to feel emotionally connected to them one last time.

Once again, though, Pia relented. She called me just a few days before the game and said I could play as long as it was only for forty-five to sixty minutes. I was grateful she'd allowed me something I wanted so badly, so I honored her wishes.

While Cal played hard, we unfortunately lost, but I cherish that last game with them. It was important for me to say good-bye and move on. Leaving college behind was hard, but it was going to be okay. I was ready to transition from college to a professional career. Playing with the national team was the next chapter of my life.

We had six days in Italy before we were due to play in Padua, just west of Venice. Italy is so beautiful, and being there brought back the wonderful memories I had of traveling there with my Cal teammates just over a year before.

Our first game against Italy started on a damp and rainy day. There were only five thousand people in the thirty-thousand-person stadium, so it wasn't exactly crowded. But a group of them were Americans from a nearby military base, and they were cheering their heads off! They were waving flags and yelling, "USA! USA!" I smiled every time I heard them.

In retaliation, the Italian fans would shoot off fireworks every now and then. It was a little jarring, but still pretty funny. Can you imagine trying to focus on something while fireworks are exploding all around you? But as the Mexican game had shown us, excited fans can make a big difference. We had to be ready for anything.

I wasn't slated to start, but I hoped and expected Pia would put me in at some point to shake things up—she had told me to be ready.

So I sat on the sidelines and watched the first half. Things were back and forth, with us dominating. We had a great shot early on from Megan Rapinoe, but the Italian goalie knocked it away. Then we almost got one in late in the first half, but again, no luck.

As we headed into the second half, Dawn Scott, our fitness coach, had told me to warm up on the sidelines.

"Alex, I think Pia's going to put you in soon," she said.

Excellent, I thought. *I'm ready.*

We were on the attack as the minutes ticked by. A few more of our shots were saved by the Italian goalie, and our goalkeeper knocked away a few herself. But still, no score.

Around the seventy-fifth minute, I could tell something was wrong with our defender Heather Mitts. I wondered, *Is she cramping up?* And sure enough, she was. Pia called her over to the sidelines and put in a sub, which left only one additional substitution for us. *Will that be me? When will I go in?* I was trying not to be anxious, but it was hard. I was *dying* to play.

"Alex, keep warming up," said Dawn. "Just be patient." So I was.

I held tight till the eighty-fifth minute, which felt like

forever, and then Pia walked up to me and looked me straight in the eye.

"You're going in now. Just go to the goal. You don't have to be tricky. You don't have to be smart. Just go to goal, because you're faster than everybody else."

If there was anything I could do, it was run fast. Remember what my club coach said? No skill, but all speed. Well, I'd learned technique since then, and I'd gotten even faster.

Just go to the goal.

For nine minutes—into stoppage time—I tried as hard as I could to do what Pia said. And then I finally got my chance. We were pushing hard toward the goal when I saw Abby, running as fast as she could, catch a long pass that she nudged off her head. It landed right in front of me, and as instructed, I ran as fast as possible. *Just go to the goal.*

I shot. And I scored.

We'd done it! We were up 1–0!

I'd had some big goals before, but this was probably the biggest of my life so far.

When the final seconds ticked away and the whistle blew, I knew we were almost there.

Just one more game, and then World Cup, here we come. . . .

Be Patient

Sometimes you just have to be patient when you're going after something. Standing on the sidelines that day in Italy, I was itching to get into the game. Eighty-five minutes felt like a lifetime! But being impatient wasn't going to help, and I knew I'd have my chance. When you're trying to achieve something, try your hardest, but be patient when things are out of your control. There's absolutely nothing you can do to speed things along, so it's best to just accept them for what they are.

CHAPTER 27

We flew home after the game with a mix of emotions—joy, relief, a little bit of nervousness, and belief in ourselves for what lay ahead. The next game against Italy was going to be held outside of Chicago, so we anticipated a friendly American crowd (with no fireworks, hopefully!). As we suited up, Pia gathered us together to give us a little pep talk.

"I know no one wanted to have to play these two games. But right now we have to look at this as though the glass is half-full. It's been a bumpy road, but we've won one game already. We need to play our hearts out and enjoy this, and it will take us all the way to Germany."

She was so right. This was *not* what we'd expected. We'd made it to the World Cup so easily in years past, and this time had been different for a million reasons. But you have to make the best of a situation when you're thrown a curveball on your path to making your dreams come true. Just look on the bright side and see the joy in the work that lies ahead of you. If you are passionate about your goals, trust me, there will be *many* moments of happiness, even if they come with lots of ups and downs along the way.

It had been bitter cold during our practices leading up to this second game, and it was thirty-one degrees on game day! This was typical for Chicago in late November, but *brrr*, it was cold. We went onto the field determined to win this game, and we hit the ground running right away. But to be honest, it wasn't our best first half. I was on the sidelines as a sub, and I watched several times as the ball slipped past the midfield, putting our defenders in a dangerous position. But as they had in the last game, they held strong, and nothing got through.

Things picked up after twenty minutes, and we started to get really aggressive, keeping the ball away from our defenders. In the fortieth minute, Megan Rapinoe dribbled the ball down the field beautifully, faked a shot, then cut back. Of course, this threw everyone off, and Megan shot. The ball hit the Italian goalkeeper, and she couldn't hold on to it. It rolled forward, and Amy Rodriguez slid right into it. The ball sailed hard into the back of the net.

We were up 1–0! At this point, the Italians would have to score two goals to even tie us in the series—three to win. This was because whoever scored the most goals between the two games was declared the winner. The way they'd been playing, things weren't looking good for them. We'd been outshooting them and keeping the ball on their side of the field much of the game. They'd have to be super aggressive to overtake us.

After the half, we headed back onto the field starting to taste victory. We weren't going to let ourselves get too comfortable, but we were definitely feeling optimistic. Amy Rodriguez had played so well that I knew chances were getting slimmer that I'd be subbed in for her, and I was going to have to be okay with that. One thing about teamwork is that you have to care for others as much as you care for yourself, so while I was eager to get on the field, standing on the sidelines and watching her dominate the game was actually kind of thrilling.

Abby was a threat the whole game too. The Italian goalkeeper was small—five-four—and Abby's five-eleven. So you can only imagine how powerful Abby seemed as she headed toward the goal time and again. It was a strong second half for us—we outshot them the whole time—and when the whistle finally blew, we'd kept the score 1–0.

The United States was going to the World Cup! It hadn't been easy, but we'd made it.

Don't Stop Believing

After we'd all hugged and congratulated the Italian team, Abby stood on the field and thanked the fans who'd braved the cold to watch us play. She mentioned that we'd never lost belief in ourselves, despite our twisty road, and that resilience and never giving up had seen us through. She is so right. Never, ever lose faith in yourself or your dreams. And never lose that fighting spirit that will make you reach your goals. If you're a fighter, you'll win.

CHAPTER 28

I had reached so many of my goals by Christmas of 2010. I had graduated college early, had played for the national team, and was poised to go to the World Cup. It wasn't guaranteed—Pia would name the team in May after a training camp—but I was feeling good about it. I was happier than I'd been in my life, but I knew that there was so much more still to do.

That's the thing about goal setting. You're really never done! But that's the fun of it. If you're a competitive, driven person, you always have another mountain to climb. Enjoy it. Your passion for what you're doing will push you forward and through all the ups and downs. And all the hard work will be worth it.

That's what I was telling myself as I faced my next challenge: the WPS college draft. Women's Professional Soccer was the US professional soccer league in place right after I graduated. There had been another league before it—the Women's United Soccer Association— but that had folded in 2003. The WPS had formed in

March 2009 with seven teams, but it was down to six teams now. It hadn't been an easy few years—only two sponsors came to the league at first, the schedules were strange with an odd number of teams, and they were losing more money than they were making.

But its existence is what counted. US women's soccer players *needed* a league to give ourselves a presence. It was important for young girls to be able to see that women were out there playing soccer and making a living from it. I remember turning on the TV when I was a kid and never seeing women. It was all baseball players and NBA stars. They weren't my idols, though— Mia Hamm and Kristine Lilly and the amazing women in the 1999 World Cup were. Communities needed the presence of professional teams to show girls that they, too, can be female athletes.

The collegiate WPS draft was on January 14, 2011. Each team looked at a pool of college players and took turns choosing whom they'd like to play for them. That day, I was on a flight to China for the Four Nations Tournament, which is an annual tournament that's been hosted by China since 1998. In 2011, few planes offered Wi-Fi, so all I could do was sit and wonder what was happening and whether I'd been chosen. As the hours ticked by, I knew a decision had been made, but I wouldn't learn what it was till I landed.

As I walked toward baggage claim after the flight, I saw our team's press officer, Aaron Heifetz. I knew something was up.

"Alex, you were the number-one collegiate pick," he said with a huge smile on his face. "You'll be playing for the Western New York Flash."

I couldn't believe it. I was the number-one pick in the draft for a professional women's soccer team. Not only would I be able to play through the winter, but I'd be part of a real league, playing with and against my senior national teammates on US soil. It was a great feeling.

The Flash started practices that winter in Rochester. That's Abby's hometown, and it was a really supportive community, but winters in Rochester are rough! It's one of the coldest and snowiest places in America, and I knew that practicing outdoors was going to be a big change from playing in California.

I was joined on the team by a few friendly faces, including Yael Averbuch, with whom I'd played on the national team. But what was really fun was how many international players there were. Christine Sinclair was one of the best forwards in Canada; Marta Vieira da Silva was a Brazilian superstar; and there were top players from Australia, Portugal, and more. I'd learned so much from playing against international players, but playing *with* them was going to be a new experience entirely.

We started the preseason in March and regular games in April. I scored the first goal in the team's inaugural game against Atlanta and a total of four goals in fourteen games. All in all, it was shaping up to be a *very* promising season.

Money Isn't Everything

If you want to succeed at something and make your dreams come true, you can't do it for money or fame. Money comes and goes, and if you watch reality TV, you know how fleeting fame can be. My starting salary with the Western New York Flash was a fraction of what a Major League Baseball rookie makes, and we often had only a few thousand fans in the stands. And TV coverage? Didn't happen. But I loved playing professionally because it was my passion, and it showed girls everywhere that women *can* play sports. So pursue your goals because *you* want them, not because you think it's going to make you rich or famous. It's what's in your heart that counts, not what's in your pockets or on TV.

CHAPTER 29

The announcement of who would be on the World Cup team was set for early May 2011. To say I was nervous would be an understatement. I'd wanted to go to the World Cup as long as I could remember. It was the biggest stage in soccer, and I'd worked my whole life for it.

I did have a good feeling. I'd really proven myself in the CONCACAF tournament, especially with my late-game goal in the first game against Italy. But I knew Pia's decision wasn't just about one goal. She looked at game performance over the last three years, watched videos from dozens of WPS games, evaluated the players at training camps, and had to look at the balance of the team. She couldn't have ten strikers, for example.

Finally, May rolled around, and twenty-one players were named. I was among them! I felt my heart swell with pride and joy. I was going to the World Cup! At twenty-one, I was the youngest player on the team, but all of us were professional players, and twelve of us were

With Jenny (left), Jeri (right), and Dad on Halloween. I was fifteen
months old. Dad took my sisters out trick or treating, and Mom and I
stayed home to hand out candy. I dressed up as a bear that year, but I
didn't have my costume on yet.

Four years old playing
T-ball with the A's, my coed
Diamond Bar team. I was
probably grinning ear to ear
because Dad was my coach.

Where it all began! My first AYSO
soccer team when I was five.

My second year in AYSO, when I was six years old. This was taken at Chaparral Middle School, across the street from my house.

With my sisters, Jenny (left) and Jeri (right), on Valentine's Day, 1997.

Celebrating with my teammate and friend Audrey after winning an AYSO game when I was seven.

Breaking away and going for the goal during an AYSO game when I was nine.

My AYSO team won the league championship when I was nine, and Mom was there to congratulate me with flowers.

With my teammates from the Diamond Heights softball league after a big win. That's me on the lower left at age ten.

My middle name is Patricia, after my aunt Patty, who's also my godmother. Aunt Patty came to watch me perform in my middle school's Christmas choir performance when I was eleven.

All speed as I dribbled the ball down the field when I was eleven. Two years later I'd start playing on a club team.

When I was in middle school, I also ran track. Here's me with my friends Tasha, Colleen, and Krista (left to right) at the San Antonio College relay races.

My coaches Eduardo (left) and Sal (right) taught me so much when I played for Cypress Elite. I'm the one wearing flip flops on the bottom row, happy as could be because we'd just won an Under-16 tournament.

Freshman year at Diamond Bar High School, my first year on the varsity team.

Playing for the Diamond Bar varsity team my junior year. Yes, I decided to go blond!

Mom and Dad came to watch me scrimmage during one of my first training camps with the US Women's National Team. We're at the StubHub Center in Carson, California, not far from where I grew up.

I love my fans! I'm reading from my book series, the Kicks, here, and some of these amazing girls were reading along with me.

Few things make me happier than working with kids. Here I am at a soccer clinic in Houston, Texas, in October 2014.

My wedding was one of the happiest days of my life. Servando and I got married in Santa Barbara on New Year's Eve, 2014.

new to the World Cup. I definitely wouldn't feel like the new kid.

I was excited to play more with the veterans. This would be the fourth World Cup for Christie Rampone, our cocaptain. (Abby is the other captain.) I'd watched her play in 1999! And Abby and Shannon Boxx were on their third World Cups. But what was so exciting was the balance of the team—everybody brought something different. As Pia said in her announcement about who'd made the cut, "We have people who organize defensively, people who can step up when it really matters, people who are good in the air, people who are fighters, and tricky ones as well." It really made me think about teamwork and the nature of a team. You're in something together, and you all have to contribute based on your individual talents. As you go after your goal, you are *nothing* without your team.

We had a few international games ahead of us—two friendly games against Japan in mid-May—and then we were meeting Mexico in an exhibition send-off match in early June. We'd fly to Austria for training camp in mid-June, and then it would all start June 28 in Germany.

Fifty days till the World Cup. Fifty days till the grandest event in all of soccer. And while I was excited every single one of those days, my life couldn't have been busier.

Pia wanted the national team to be together as much as possible, so she set up a camp in Florida. When we weren't with our club teams, we were expected to be at camp training, getting to know our teammates and mentally preparing for the World Cup.

But on the weekends, I'd fly to Buffalo or somewhere else in the country to play for the Flash. I'd play, then say good-bye to my teammates and get back on a plane for Florida.

If you've spent a lot of time traveling, you know how stressful it can be. You have to pack carefully, dash to the airport, wait in lines, and hope your luggage gets to your destination at the same time you do. Now, imagine doing that twice a week, sometimes three or four times! Often I forgot what time zone I was living in.

Most of the national team was doing this, too, since almost everyone played on a club team. So while I wasn't alone, that didn't make it any easier. I felt stretched so thin, like I was living two different lives.

But I was doing it for the sake of something great, and that was the World Cup. Realizing that made all the stress worthwhile.

Make Sacrifices

When you're chasing after your dreams, you may have to skip important events in your life because of your commitments. You might have debate tournaments every weekend, so you miss a school dance, leaving behind what feels like a huge part of your high school experience. But pursuing your goals often necessitates making sacrifices, so it's something you just have to learn to deal with. That was the case for me in early 2011. Personal time just didn't happen—I'd had to let it go to meet my soccer commitments. If you're going through something like this, just know that it's probably not permanent, and keep the big picture in mind: You're going after your goals.

CHAPTER 30

June 28 arrived, and we were all on pins and needles. We were set to play our first game against North Korea, and while we didn't think it was going to be a terribly difficult game, we weren't taking anything for granted.

Unfortunately, I wasn't on the starting roster. My late-game save in the qualifying game against Italy hadn't yet convinced Pia that I was suited to be a starter. At that point, my strength lay in last-minute heroics.

But it was okay. Pia had always taught us to accept our roles on the team, whatever they were. Mine was to come off the bench and make an immediate impact. She wanted me to run at the opponent's defenders and tire them out. I knew that when Pia felt the team needed me as a starter, she'd put me in.

When you're pursuing your dreams, sometimes you just have to accept the role you play on a team and realize you may not always—or ever—be the star. If you play gymnastics, you may not win an individual competition, but your team might win overall. Never forget that your contributions helped that happen. Winning may be *your* dream, but if it's tied to a team, sometimes you have to take a backseat to the group as a whole. That was me at the start of the World Cup.

The entire Cup was being held in nine cities in Germany. The way the tournament works is that the sixteen teams in the tournament play in several rounds, the first being the group stage. There are four groups consisting of four teams, and each team plays three games within their group. You get points in each game—three points for a win, one for a draw, and none for a loss. The two teams with the most points at the end of the group stage advance to the knockout stage: the quarterfinals, then the semi-finals, then the finals. There are no ties in these games. You play till you win, and if you lose, you go home.

The night of June 28 in Dresden, Germany, was hot and steamy. As I sat on the sidelines and listened to the starting whistle blow, I felt so great. This was a huge sporting event and the culmination of so many of my dreams, and I was there.

The first half was scoreless, but midway through the second half we got on the board. Abby made a terrific pass to Lauren Cheney, and she headed the ball into the left side of the goal. And then North Korea went on the attack—they made a great shot from about twenty-five feet that would have gone in if it hadn't hit the top of the goalpost. Goal averted! We were so relieved.

The first half came and went, and I got more and more eager to get into the game. *Soon*, I told myself. Then, in the seventy-fourth minute, I got my chance. One of our four forwards, Amy Rodriguez, had just made a fantastic shot that forced a save, but Pia decided to pull her out of the game. It was my turn to shake things up. I stood up, just a little nervous and a lot excited, and I adjusted my pink headband. *Lucky thirteen, here you go.*

When Amy approached the sideline, I broke into a run, darting across the field. *I made it. I was about to turn twenty-two years old, and I was playing in the World Cup.*

Just one minute later we were on the board again. Rachel Buehler, who was also making her World Cup debut, caught a pass from Carli Lloyd and kicked it right past three Korean defenders to get it over the line. GOAL!

North Korea couldn't come back after that, so we finished the game with a final score of 2–0. It was a thrilling start to my first World Cup, and I couldn't have been happier that I'd been on the field to see us clinch the victory.

With a 3–0 victory against Colombia in our next game in the group stage, we secured our spot in the quarterfinals. In the group stage of the World Cup, if you win two games, you're in. But the victory was bittersweet. It was my twenty-second birthday, and I hadn't been given the chance to play.

I was subbed in at halftime for our next game against Sweden, though. We lost 2–1, which was a disappointment because it ended our twenty-year unbeaten streak in the group stage, but we couldn't dwell on it too long— we were still going to the quarterfinals.

And that's where our real test would begin. . . .

Move On

After the game against Colombia, I was a little more morose than I usually am. I'd wanted to play on my birthday *so badly*, and I felt overlooked. I needed twenty-four hours to get over my disappointment, which was always my rule. You get twenty-four hours to sulk and feel sorry for yourself, but after the day is over, you move on and look forward. I think this is a good rule—twenty-four hours is actually a *long* time! You can do a lot of sulking in a day. Feel your pain, then move on to bigger and better things.

CHAPTER 31

If someone had told me what our quarterfinal game against Brazil was going to be like, I'm not sure I would have been so laid-back about our loss to Sweden. Even Pia was relaxed!

"I thought it was a good game today: entertaining but also tactically pretty interesting," Pia said in an interview after the Sweden game. "I think we'll get stronger, and it will be inspiring to play against Brazil." See? Confident and chill. Whew! The Brazil game was anything but.

Unless you've been living in a cave, you know how important soccer is to Brazil. You can go to a town there that has fewer than one hundred people and no running water—but they'll have a soccer field. Their superstar forward, Marta Vieira da Silva, who was my Flash teammate (just called "Marta" because in Brazil all footballers use only their first names), had been the FIFA player of the year five years running. But Brazil had never won a major tournament. In fact, they'd lost to us in the

Olympic gold-medal game twice. Long story short, they had something to prove.

It started off well—no, really well—when Shannon Boxx crossed the ball over to Abby within the first minute and a half of play, and one of the Brazilian players accidentally knocked it in.

"It's in! It's in!" I heard a few girls yell from the sidelines. Pia threw her hands up and jumped into the air.

Kicking the ball into your own team's goal is called an own goal, and it's always awful when it happens. I mean, awful to the person who does it. For us it was great!

But that own goal must have strengthened Brazil's resolve to make us suffer. I wasn't a starter, so I was sitting on the sidelines for that first half, watching them get more and more aggressive as the game went on. They didn't take any shots on goal in the first twenty minutes, but then, bam, they took four in less than ten minutes. We went into halftime with the edge—the score was still 1–0—but the lead felt really fragile.

At halftime Pia worked as hard as possible to pump us up.

"We all know how Brazil plays," she said. "We can't give up any stupid fouls. We know their antics—they'll make the most of them. And they will dive for balls. They will claw their way back. We need to control the tempo of the game, and we need to keep the ball!"

She could not have been more right. In the sixty-fifth minute, the tide of the game suddenly turned. Marta and Rachel Buehler were battling it out inside our penalty box, with Rachel doing a great job of holding Marta back from scoring. With Rachel right there, Marta shot for the goal—and missed. She fell to the ground and began rolling around, supposedly in pain. Aha! These were the antics Pia had mentioned.

The whistle blew, and we all couldn't believe it when Rachel was given a red card.

"What? No way!" yelled Pia. We were shocked. A red card? How was it possible that Rachel was leaving the game on a penalty none of us had seen? We found out later the referee had ruled that Rachel had fouled Marta in the penalty box, so Brazil was given a penalty kick.

The kicker belted it . . . and Hope Solo knocked it away. Amazing!

But then the whistle blew again, and the referee pulled out a yellow card and waved it at Hope. What? We questioned the ref immediately.

"The goalkeeper moved off the goal line before the shot was made. Brazil gets to take another penalty kick," she responded.

We were in disbelief. Again, none of us had seen this. Was the ref just against us?

After the game, this call was changed. The officials

ruled that Hope hadn't moved off the line, but instead Christie Rampone had entered the penalty box before the ball was kicked. While knowing we were right felt good, it was bittersweet. No matter what, we still would have had a penalty shot taken against us.

Brazil lined up at the penalty marker and kicked. And this time Hope just couldn't stop it. We were tied 1–1.

Not having Rachel on the field meant we were now down to ten players, which was bad news. And we had a huge chip on our shoulders—we'd just had two penalties given to us that we flat-out disagreed with. But we couldn't let ourselves be beaten.

"Alex, you're up," Pia finally said in the seventy-second minute. I was thrilled. No longer would I watch helplessly. I was going in, and I was going to help us win.

I took a deep breath and vowed to play my best. But it wasn't easy. I played hard, and although I felt I'd contributed to the team, we weren't able to score again. Regulation time ended, and we were still tied 1–1 with Brazil.

As we prepared for thirty minutes of extra time—two fifteen-minute periods—a swell of cheers for Team USA arose from the crowd. They clearly felt we'd been wronged.

Unfortunately, Brazil scored first, and they scored fast. And yet again, it was based on a bad call—or lack of a call—by the ref. Early on in extra time, a Brazilian player who was clearly offside made a pass to Marta, and Marta kicked it right in the goal.

We had to claw back into the game against all odds—still with only ten players. But sometimes when you're playing hard and playing well, doubling your effort is easy.

We were far into the second period of extra time, the score still 2–1, when we really kicked it into overdrive. The ref had added three minutes of extra time, and the chants of "USA, USA!" were practically shaking the stands. I don't think the crowd felt we were underdogs. I think they wanted us to win because of the bad calls that had put us into the position we were in.

I looked over and saw Abby pointing up with one finger, like she was directing us to look at the sky. But it wasn't that. She was signaling the number one.

"One chance! One moment! That's all it takes!" She was screaming at the top of her lungs. "All it takes is one chance!"

She was so right. Sometimes things can change in an instant. And with only a few minutes left in the game, what happened next was going to prove that to us and to the world.

Megan was taking the ball down the field, running faster than I'd ever seen. She kicked from far behind the penalty box, and Abby jumped in the air next to two defenders. The ball made contact with her head, and it sailed into the goal. At 122 minutes in the game, when we were a minute away from the earliest elimination from the World Cup we'd ever had, Abby did what Abby does best: She headed a goal.

Extra time came to an end, and once again we were tied, 2–2. It was on to penalty shots.

I knew we had momentum on our side. We'd scored in the 122nd minute, so we were riding high. Brazil wasn't. They'd just seen victory slip through their fingers.

We shot, then Brazil shot, then back again with no misses until the third Brazilian player—the poor soul who'd made the own goal in the first half—kicked . . . and missed! If we scored two more penalty kicks, we'd win.

And sure enough, we did it! We made all five shots just perfectly, and we were on to the semifinals by the skin of our teeth.

Keep a Level Head

No matter how well you're succeeding, things may become *really* messed up. Someone might betray you, or you may be accused of something you didn't do. But you can't lose your cool. Pia could have run onto the field screaming and waving her arms when Hope and Rachel were given penalty cards, but then *she* would have been thrown out of the game. And we needed her. So keep calm and carry on—a level head will allow you to keep going.

CHAPTER 32

In many ways, the semifinal game against France was going to be a battle of the old guard versus the new. It's funny. Even though we were the best team in the world and had won the World Cup twice, we were still considered the new guys because soccer is less of a tradition in the United States. I'd never been to France, but I knew how important culture and art are to them—from cuisine to museums to sports. They play soccer like they cook—with finesse, technique, patience, and style. We have that too, but we are better known for our fitness, power, and speed.

Again Pia hadn't tapped me as a starter, and I trusted her decision. For the past two games I'd come out explosively in the second half and really boosted the energy of the team. They were calling me "Baby Horse," which was kind of funny. "Baby" because I was so young and "Horse" because I have a long stride and practically gallop across the field.

It was a gray and misty day in Frankfurt, totally

unlike the game against Brazil, when we were positively sweating because it was so hot. We went out on the field strong, and Lauren Cheney scored fast—in the ninth minute. But I remembered not to be too confident. We'd gotten on the board within two minutes in the game against Brazil, and look how that turned out!

France came back strong, and they were really putting pressure on our defenders. Rachel Buehler was still suspended from the red card she'd received in the last game, so Becky Sauerbrunn was taking her place on defense. Unlike the last game, this meant we now had eleven players again. The defense had to work hard, and Hope made some saves that took my breath away. If anyone doubted her, between this game and the Brazil game, she'd proven that she was the best goalkeeper in the sport.

France finally scored ten minutes into the second half, tying the game at 1–1. I don't think they'd worn our defense down. They just had a lucky shot that Hope couldn't catch.

That's when I went in.

"Alex, it's your turn. You're subbing for Amy Rodriguez," said Pia. That had become a kind of theme for me—go in during the second half for Amy, push and run like crazy, control the ball, and allow the other players to score. As fun as that was, I was dying to get a goal myself. I wanted to show the world that I was more than just Baby Horse.

But it was Abby who was going to strike first, and she made another one of her famous headers to score in the seventy-ninth minute. Lauren Cheney made a high, soaring cross from the right side to the left post, and Abby just bumped it right in.

GOAL! We were up 2–1.

Three minutes later, it was my turn. After a series of quick plays, Megan took control of the ball, and when she saw me ahead of her, to the right, she jabbed the ball toward me with her right foot. I was waiting, and I put my legs in motion and burst away from defender who had been on my back. I was fast, and I was on my own, approaching the goalkeeper inside the penalty box.

In that moment, I remembered all the shots on goal I'd taken with my dad. We'd practiced finishing so much—*take the ball to the goal, aim, and fire.* Dad always taught me to focus with laserlike intensity on getting the ball into the net, and that's what I did right then. I watched the goalie sliding down toward the ground, as if she was anticipating that I was about to kick, and then I took the ball right over her.

It hit the back of the net and made a giant *swooooosh.*

I can't remember exactly what was going through my head at that moment. Excitement, I'm sure. Disbelief?

Probably not. Because I'd known I could do it. As Abby had said in the game against Brazil, I just needed one opportunity. I'd gotten it, and were going to the World Cup finals.

Seize Every Opportunity

We closed out our game against France 3–1. I had dreamed of making a goal in the World Cup since I was a little girl, and finally, I'd done it. But when you're going after your goals, it's important to remember what Abby said: Big things can happen in *just one moment*. One decision (like me deciding exactly where to aim my shot) can make all the difference between you making a goal and missing it, so seize every opportunity and never slack off.

CHAPTER 33

I 've talked a lot about patience in this book, but I can't stress it enough. Sometimes the culmination of your dreams takes time. *A lot* of time. It had been twelve years since the United States had been to a World Cup final, let alone won one, as the twenty-one of us were all too aware. We had the biggest game of our careers ahead of us, and we had no choice but to win. We'd worked too hard and overcome too much to do anything less.

We had traveled from Dresden to Frankfurt after our win against France, and we were set to play Japan in the final. While we were determined to win, our hearts were bleeding for Japan. That March, a devastating earthquake and tsunami struck the country and killed more than fifteen thousand people, so the Japanese people were still reeling. The press was hailing the Japanese women's team's success to this point as a Cinderella story. After all the loss and devastation to their country and people, they seemed to have a certain strength willing them into the World Cup final.

When we'd played Japan in May before the World Cup, we'd held an auction. We autographed all our jerseys and sold them online, raising more than twenty thousand dollars, which went to the Red Cross for tsunami relief. It was the least we could do—you *have* to help out when something so terrible happens. People need you if you're in a position to help.

Historically, Japan hadn't been a formidable opponent. They'd never beaten us. In fact, they'd lost twenty-two times against us and tied three times, and we'd outscored them 77–13. But after seeing them knock out Germany in the quarterfinals and beat Sweden in the semifinals, we'd developed a lot of respect for them. And Pia warned us about how technical their game could be. They were incredibly precise, which we'd seen in our May games against them. Plus, we'd learned we couldn't take anything for granted after the qualifying tournament game against Mexico. Teams you don't think can win can rally and wear you down. As you go after your goals, you have to be aware of that—just because an opponent isn't as good as you doesn't mean they can't beat you.

The world's sympathies may have been with Japan, but we had a game to play, and we could be supportive and still play a good game of soccer. So when we took the field in front of more than forty-eight thousand people, the chants of "USA! USA!" may have seemed a little quieter than in other games, but we weren't going to let that get us down. Even with only one player on our team having a World Cup title under her belt (Christie Rampone), we believed this was our year. For the amount of talent we had, we knew we had to go out and get the title and bring it home. We knew we were the better team; we just had to execute.

Pia had made two changes to the starting lineup, an unusual move for her. Megan Rapinoe had played so well in the previous games—that incredible cross to Abby in the 122nd minute of the game against Brazil was still fresh in everyone's mind—so Pia put her in to start. And Rachel Buehler was back after her one-game red-card suspension, so she was itching to play. Of course, I was too, but I'd have to wait until the second half.

We filed out onto the field, and my heart swelled as I saw the crowd. There were American flags everywhere, and I realized right then I'd never played in front of so many people. My family was up there, and all my friends at home were watching. I'd gotten e-mails and texts from people I hadn't seen in years! This was the culmination of everything I'd ever worked for, but I had to remember it wasn't about me. This was a team effort, and not just the national team. It was the result of every team we'd ever played on.

The whistle blew and the ball began to move. *This was it.*

We started off like we'd been shot out of a gun, but so did the Japanese. Lauren Cheney, who was playing forward since Megan had taken over the midfield, shot in the first thirty seconds, but the Japanese goalie kicked it out of the way. Still, I was really impressed by Lauren's intensity and how quickly she'd taken a shot on goal.

Within fifteen minutes of playing, I could tell Megan was on fire. She'd made a beautiful cross to Lauren that she failed to get in (it was *so close*), and three minutes later, she took a strong shot that was deflected just wide. Her long passes were amazing, and in the eighteenth minute she made an incredibly powerful kick that would have gone in if it hadn't hit the left goalpost.

But let's not forget Abby, who'd saved us time and again throughout the tournament. I watched with amazement in the thirtieth minute as she drove the ball from midfield, moving it within striking distance of the goal, and made a mind-blowing shot to the goal that bounced off the crossbar. *Darn!* It was so close to going in.

At that point, my relationship with Abby was rock solid. We anticipated each other's runs, passes, and moves on the field. We thought on the same wavelength, as if we'd been playing together for much longer than just two years. We were happy when we were up front together, and our positive energy made us play with power and incredible style. Right then I missed being on the field with her.

As I stood on the sidelines watching the game, Japan didn't seem to be as threatening as I'd expected. Yes, they were technical, and yes, they were fast, but we'd had more shots on goal and been far more dominant. They didn't even really take a shot till the thirty-first minute, but that failed to go in.

So when we went into the locker room at halftime, part of me was surprised the game was scoreless. We'd played so powerfully, so why weren't we winning?

Fortunately, I'd have a chance to see firsthand. Lauren had sprained her ankle early on in the game, but she'd gritted her teeth through forty-five minutes of play. By halftime, she had to rest.

As I walked onto the field at the beginning of the second half, I knew the pressure was on. My family was up there in the stands, but that was down near the bottom of my concerns—they'd love me no matter what. This was the *World Cup*, and the hopes and dreams of our country were resting on our shoulders.

Then again, the same held true for Japan, and possibly even more so. Japan had suffered unimaginable horrors since March, and a win would help them heal.

But we had to put that all out of our minds for now. This was a competition, after all.

When the starting whistle blew, Japan sprang into action right away. They were fast and playing hard, and we could all tell they were hungry. But I got my big moment early on. In the forty-ninth minute I had charged into the penalty area and was standing inches from the goal. Heather O'Reilly brought the ball down the field and crossed it over to me. I caught the ball, gained control, and shot.

BOOM! It hit the post. What a letdown.

Then Abby almost headed a ball into the goal twenty minutes later, but it wasn't to be—the ball tipped off the goalkeeper's fingers and went soaring over the top of the bar.

It felt like the game was going to go on like this forever. When would we score? It was almost seventy minutes into regulation, we'd taken twice as many shots as Japan, and we still hadn't gotten on the board. Was destiny not on our side?

Thankfully, all those negative thoughts went away in the sixty-ninth minute. I was in the midfield, waiting for my chance while watching a huge scramble for the ball down in our penalty area. It was four-on-one—four of our players versus one of theirs—and Carli Lloyd untangled the ball, kicking it right to Megan.

Megan had been a superstar this entire game, making long, precise passes. Her legs move in the weirdest ways (that's why we call her "Gumby!"), allowing her to send balls through the air better than anyone. She gained control of the ball, saw me *way* down the field, and kicked it fifty yards. The ball landed a little to my left and just slightly behind me, but it bounced and rolled fast, and I sprinted to it. I reached the ball, dribbled it into the penalty box with a Japanese defender hot on my tail, and then I shot with my left foot.

It sailed into the goal. It was a perfect finish, and with that, I'd scored the first goal of the World Cup final.

When I pulled myself off the ground, the first person to hug me was Abby. *Is this a dream?* I thought. *Or did I really just score in the World Cup final?* When I heard the crowd explode, I knew it was real. I thought of all the coaches and teammates I'd had along the way and all the hard practices and late nights studying so I could clear my schedule for a game. As I've said before, one moment of happiness like this makes every drop of sweat and every tear you've shed in your life worth it. Success is the best feeling in the world.

We would have celebrated more, but we had a game to play! So we scrambled back to the center of the field.

After ten minutes of play, the eightieth minute came way too fast, and unfortunately, a mistake on our part led to Japan scoring the tying goal. We tried to clear the ball away from the box, but we couldn't do it, and the ball bounced *closer* to the goal, toward our defender Ali Krieger. Ali tried desperately to get it away, but it hit a Japanese player named Aya Miyami, and she tapped it right in from four yards away. It wasn't Ali's fault—these things happen—but I'm sure she felt terrible.

If we could score in the next ten minutes, we'd likely win, but our continued hard work didn't pay off. Regulation ended with us still tied 1–1, and there were mixed emotions all around. This was our second over-time in three games, and that's a lot. We were tired, but we were determined to win. As I've said before, we never give up, because things can change in an instant.

Abby had a few chances to score early in overtime, but it wasn't till the 102nd minute that she actually did it. And it was from an assist by me! I passed her the ball from inside the penalty box, and she headed it right in. GOAL! We were up 2–1—so close to winning.

I wish that had ended the game, but it hadn't. We still had a second overtime that was fifteen minutes long, and while the minutes ticked away I nervously antici-pated the end of the game. But in the 117th minute, Japan struck. They took a corner kick that landed per-fectly inside the goal box, and when one of their players attacked the ball, it bounced right off Abby and sailed past Hope. There was nothing Hope or Abby could have done—it wasn't an own goal and it wasn't a mistake. It was just a lucky kick.

With that we were tied 2–2. Overtime ended, and we were going to penalty kicks.

Shannon Boxx was up first. This was Shannon's second World Cup, and while I knew she must have been nervous, she was a veteran and a professional. We could depend on her.

She shot, and the Japanese goalie dove to the left, deflecting the ball off her foot. *We'd missed*. This was not a good start.

But remember, things can change in an instant, and it was Japan's turn to kick. They set the ball down, ran for it, shot . . . and scored. We were down 1–0 in penalties.

It was our turn again, and our hearts were in our throats as Carli Lloyd went up to the line. *C'mon, Carli*, I thought to myself. She paused for a moment and moved toward the ball. Her kick was high . . . and it sailed over the top. Carli put her hand over her wide-open mouth, like she was either shocked or was going to be sick. We knew how she felt—this had gone from bad to worse.

But again, things can change in an instant, and while we were down 2–1 in penalty shots, Japan could still miss, and we'd have a chance to climb back. It was still early.

The Japanese player put the ball on the penalty mark, backed up, ran toward the ball, kicked . . . and as it sailed toward Hope, I saw her dive for it. She saved it! We were back!

Then it was Tobin Heath's turn. Tobin has become one of my closest friends, and she's a powerful presence on the field. But she was subbing for Megan Rapinoe here, and she was feeling the weight of the world on her shoulders.

She put the ball on the mark, ran toward it, and kicked it right into the goalie's hands. Tobin looked to be in utter disbelief. As the player next to me gripped my hands harder, I realized we were *all* in utter disbelief.

This was so uncharacteristic of us. We *never* missed kicks in a shoot-out, and here we were, having missed three in a row. Carli's kick had been completely off, and Tobin's had just been weak. What had happened?

There was no time to think as the Japanese kicker came to the line. She shot, the ball sailed toward the goal, and Hope dove for it. She got her hands on it, but she couldn't keep it out. Japan had scored. Our spirits sank lower.

Now, at this point we had to score or we'd lose the game. Abby was up next, and looking like she'd done this a thousand times, she put the ball down, kicked, and scored, making it all seem so easy. She ran back toward us with a serious look, then pumped her hands, as if she'd forgotten to celebrate. *That was right. It wasn't over.*

Hope took a bit of time getting back to the goal for the next penalty kick. The Japanese player was ready, but Hope was making her wait. If Japan got this in, it was over. I knew she needed time to collect herself.

The ball sailed high, and it was a beautiful shot, spinning just slightly as it went over Hope's head. I heard Japan begin to scream and saw their sidelined players run onto the field, and I knew it was over. There was nothing Hope could have done. The game was all Japan's.

We had lost the World Cup in penalty kicks, and it was time to go home.

I can't describe the sadness and disappointment we felt. We'd worked so hard, and we'd come so far. Losing in a dramatic fashion like that is a shock to your system, and everyone feels responsible.

I walked to the stands, where my parents, my sister Jeri, and my aunt were waiting for me. I was crying, hugging them, and just looking for a little comfort. There was nothing they could say to change what had happened, but being with them made me feel just the tiniest bit of peace.

It would take me days and weeks to process it all, and in many ways I still am. But all you can do is pick yourself up and move on to the next game. Which is what I planned to do. We'd learn something from this, and we'd be back.

Don't Blame Yourself

Losing or failing is the most difficult thing in the whole world. When you work so hard for something, not making your goal feels like a death. There's no satisfaction, only pain. It's easy to blame yourself for the mistakes you made—and believe me, we made a lot in the World Cup—but kicking yourself isn't worth it. Blame gets you nowhere. Just try to learn something from the mistakes you made and try to do things differently next time.

CHAPTER 34

After the World Cup I hadn't expected to feel as mentally drained as I did. I knew I'd be physically tired, but the emotional side was a whole different thing. I gave myself time to let that pass, and eventually, it did. I didn't embrace the pain—I just let it be—and it finally went away of its own accord.

The press was very kind to us, and we got a lot more support than I'd expected. I thought we'd receive criticism from some people and sympathy from others, but instead the press and fans were proud of us. I wasn't happy to come home in second place, but our fans didn't turn against us, and I was grateful for that. I'm sure there were some people who were critical, but I missed it, thankfully. We couldn't have fought harder than we did in the World Cup, and most people saw that.

It also seemed like people were pretty happy for Japan. Even President Barack Obama sent Japan his congratulations, tweeting,

Congratulations to Japan, women's World Cup champions.

Thankfully, he added that he couldn't be prouder of the women of the US national team after a hard-fought game.

He was right, and I had to remember that. We had fought hard. We had played hard. And we'd played as a team, with each and every player contributing to the beautiful goals we'd made, the heroic saves, and the next-to-impossible assists.

My goal for the World Cup had been to win, and that didn't happen, but I quickly realized that it wasn't the end of the world. Goals can be missed—on the field and in life—and it's what you learn from it that counts.

Plus, I'd met lots of my goals along the way—score a World Cup goal (I'd scored two!), make a World Cup assist, and prove that I wasn't just some twenty-two-year-old kid fresh out of college. Well, I *was* a twenty-two-year-old fresh out of college, but I wasn't a kid. I'd shown real maturity on the field, and I wasn't just Baby Horse anymore.

"I think she's a stallion now," said Megan Rapinoe.

When I went home, I went back to playing for the Western New York Flash. In fact, I had a match within three days after the final against Japan! I was tired but ready to get on the field again. Maybe it would help me forget what happened at the World Cup final.

Day by day, it did help. And at the end of August, I felt *really* good because we were set to play the Philadelphia Independence in the championship Women's Professional Soccer game. There were more than ten thousand people in attendance, which showed how much women's soccer in the United States had exploded since the World Cup. While it might have been a fraction of the number of people who were at the World Cup final, it was a record for a Women's Professional Soccer final.

I played for 104 minutes, and we went into overtime. It seemed like a theme in my life at this point! We were so evenly matched with Philadelphia—both offensively and defensively—and it was a lot of back and forth the first half, with no one scoring.

The hilarious thing that happened early in the first half—much-needed comic relief, since we were all a little jumpy—was that a squirrel ran onto the field and wouldn't get off. It ran in a little circle in the penalty box, just going around and around and at one point dragging its stomach and back legs along the ground. Finally, an official had to come onto the field with a box and drag it off. You can watch it on YouTube—it's got more than three hundred thousand views, in fact.

Christine Sinclair—our captain and one of Canada's best players—finally scored for us in the second half, and we thought for sure we'd won until Amy Rodriguez, my teammate from the national team, scored for the Independence with two minutes left in regulation. You might remember that Amy was the forward I kept subbing for during the World Cup. She's a great player, and even though I wish she hadn't scored, I was impressed by what a good goal it was.

After two sets of extra time during which no one scored, we went to penalty kicks. We scored all five of our goals, though I didn't shoot since I'd been subbed out at that point. Philadelphia had made four out of their five when their last kicker went up. She shot . . . and she missed.

The Flash won! I think even the squirrel was excited.

My first year of professional soccer was wonderful in so many ways. I played with international players, I learned a tremendous amount from a new coach, and I loved training every day.

Unfortunately, the WPS folded in May 2012. We were incredibly disappointed, but we weren't surprised. There were a lot of mistakes, bad decisions, and unfortunate events that had happened throughout the WPS's short history: One of the team owners filed a lawsuit against the league; some teams were paying players much higher salaries than other teams, so owners were seeing big losses at the end of each season; and many teams kept switching owners, which would cause the team to have to rebrand itself. All of these issues led to major financial troubles.

This was a blow to all of us. The WPS had been the second US women's soccer league to shut down, and we all wondered what the future held for professional soccer. We were an international powerhouse. Why couldn't we be one in our own country? And ten thousand people had shown up for the championship. Didn't that mean something?

I made a promise to help advance professional soccer for women. I'd do everything in my power to help elevate it to the place it deserved. People should be watching it on TV every weekend! I could help them by playing my best with my teammates and winning games. The more exciting the games and the higher the level of play, the more people would attend games and the more money would flow into the sport. Soccer was too important to too many young women to let it fall by the wayside.

Distractions Can Help

Returning to the United States after the World Cup loss was hard, but I began to feel better when I joined the Western New York Flash again. Playing with them distracted me from the pain I was feeling from the loss. I didn't forget what had happened, but at least I was able to focus on something different. If you've missed a goal or experienced a loss, try to actively engage in something, if only for a little bit. If you didn't get a part in a play, dive into another school activity. Or if you failed a test, try to study extra hard in another class. Doing well at something else may just lift your spirits.

CHAPTER 35

Sometimes when you have so much going on in your life your relationships can fall by the wayside. I think this is okay if those relationships are destructive or don't add much to your life, but you can never, ever forget the people who've been wonderful to you along the way. Remember: You didn't get to where you are by yourself—those relationships helped get you there!

It had been hard being away from Servando so much. We hadn't lived in the same city for more than a year. He'd been at Cal while I was training for the Olympics, and then he'd gone to Seattle to play professionally for the Sounders. We talked all the time, but it wasn't the same.

What was especially hard was that while we were both playing soccer, doing what we loved, we were in different places in life in many ways. We just had so much going on that didn't involve each other—him a professional career and me the World Cup. Our day-to-day lives didn't consist of the basic things that keep couples on the same page—from going out with the same friends to grocery shopping together.

There was tension in our relationship. We'd always been so close, and suddenly, our lives had diverged. What was happening to us?

The worst thing you can do in a relationship is not talk about something that's causing problems. When you don't talk, the problem just gets bigger, and you start feeling tense or fighting. So one day we decided to have a conversation about it, and it made things much better. We realized we both loved each other and wanted to support each other no matter what—if we were in different cities, if one of us was more famous or making more money than the other, whatever. We just wanted to be together. And ultimately, that was what was important!

Little did I know that Servando was also campaigning to get me to come to Seattle. He didn't just want us to stay together; he wanted us to *be* together. When the WPS folded, I'd been left without a team. But the Sounders had a semiprofessional women's team, so Servando began to talk to the general manager about bringing me over. She loved the idea, and one day she called me.

Of course, I accepted immediately.

Servando and I would be in the same city for the first time in more than a year. We could wear the same jerseys, we could go to each other's games, and best of all, we could go on dates like a normal couple. No more late-night phone calls in different time zones, no more missing each other every second of every day. We could be together for real. It was wonderful for both of us.

Going to the Sounders was also a reunion with the national team—Hope Solo, Megan Rapinoe, Stephanie Cox, and Sydney Leroux played for them. I had missed these women terribly, and playing with them again felt like going home. It also gave us the chance to remember what made us such a good team and work out some of the kinks that had held us back in the previous year.

And Seattle is a terrific sports town—they *love* their soccer teams. Even though I got to play in only three games that year because of my commitments with the national team, the Sounders women sold out nine out of their ten games, and attendance at the games was four times higher than the next team in the league. We felt supported and loved, and all in all, it was a perfect bridge to the Olympic qualifying tournament.

Surrounded by people I loved, I headed toward the next goal in my life. . . .

Protect Your Relationships

I can't stress enough how important it is to keep good relationships in your life as you make your dreams come true. But you have to nurture these relationships—they do take work. If I hadn't talked to Servando about our problems, we would have had even more issues. Take time each day to think about the people in your life you love, and tell them how much you need them. They will appreciate it—I promise.

CHAPTER 36

My big goal at the beginning of the national team season in January 2012 was to get on to the starting lineup, and I was ready to work as hard as I needed to get there.

The season started off with another CONCACAF qualifying tournament, this time for the 2012 Olympics to be held that summer in London. If we qualified for the Olympics, Pia would name the Olympic roster in late May, a little more than a month before the games.

Being back with the national team was wonderful. Most of the bad feelings from last year's World Cup had passed, and we were all feeling bullish about the games ahead. And it's funny to say, but we were just a *better* team. Maybe going through such a tough time had made us stronger. Oftentimes, that's the case.

The tournament was occurring over ten days in Vancouver at the end of January. Like at the World Cup qualifying tournament, there were eight teams, and the first- and second-place winners were guaranteed a spot at the Olympics.

I won't go into too much detail about the early games except to say that it was some of the best soccer of our lives, and we were playing *completely* as a team. We had grown so much since the World Cup, building from our mistakes and becoming even stronger. We steamrolled the competition in the group stage, beating the Dominican Republic 14–0, then defeating Guatemala 13–0! We shut out Mexico 4–0 in the last game of the group stage, which felt particularly sweet in light of our loss to them in the World Cup qualifying tournament. But it wasn't about redemption. We just wanted to keep winning.

Then we dominated Costa Rica 4–0 in the semifinals, which secured our spot in the Olympics.

We hadn't doubted that we'd be going to the Olympics, but to do it so decisively felt great. We were a scoring machine, and we didn't give up a single goal in those early games, showing that our defense was stronger than ever. I was so proud of the way we'd played, and I was honored to be in the company of such powerhouse players. As for going to the Olympics? While I wasn't guaranteed to be on the roster, all indications were that I would be. The thought of it was a dream come true.

But despite how dominant we'd been, I still hadn't

been named a starter, and I was getting antsy. Did Pia not want to change things around since we'd been playing so well lately? Or was I just too important as a late-game weapon? Either way, the decision was out of my hands, so I vowed to be patient. I knew I'd get there.

The day before the next game, the final against Canada, I had one of the best practices of my life. Every shot I took went in, and every play I made was perfect. I began to have the strangest feeling. I sensed a voice deep inside me whispering that tomorrow could be my first-ever start with the team.

And then Pia pulled me aside after training and started talking to me.

"Alex, you've been working really hard, and you've proven yourself on this team. I'm proud of all that you've done."

I began to smile. Pia hadn't *exactly* said that I'd be starting, but her words fueled my hope.

Sure enough, when the starting lineup was named the night before the game, there I was.

See? Everything can change in an instant. I felt like I'd arrived. All that training, all that hard work, and here it was, the end of January, and I'd made my goal. Now I just had to prove that Pia had made the right decision.

• • •

The final of the Olympic qualifying tournament was held in Vancouver on January 29, 2012, and in front of a record crowd that topped twenty-five thousand people, we beat Canada on their home turf.

Our 4–0 victory was a testament to how well Abby and I played together. Pia had put us in a 4-4-2 formation, so I was up front as a striker alongside Abby. This was the first time we had started together, and I think that day marks the official beginning of the beautiful soccer we've been playing together ever since.

I got a goal in the fourth minute off an assist from Abby, and then Abby scored in the twenty-fourth and twenty-eighth minutes off assists from me. But what was so exciting was that Abby's second goal marked her 131st career goal, which surpassed Kristine Lilly's second-place record. Abby was behind Mia Hamm as the second-highest scorer in US history! We were thrilled for her—she'd worked her heart out for this—and I was so honored to have helped her get there.

But despite how well I was playing, I still felt like I had so much to learn, even about very basic game tactics. Don't feel bad if you find yourself feeling as inexperienced as I did. It's totally normal, and usually there's someone to help you through it. For me, that person was Abby. I remember looking at her, confused, after the third goal in the second half and saying, "So where do we go from here?"

Abby's such a veteran that she didn't have to think twice when she responded to me. "Our work's not finished yet," she replied. She was right: We had to keep fighting. What she'd told me was a fundamental lesson, but I needed to hear it at that moment. You can't let up till the final whistle blows.

We did just as Abby said: We never stopped. In the second half, Canada had a few chances to score, but we were just too strong. And in the fifty-sixth minute, I made one more goal. Soon the whistle blew.

We had won the tournament, proving to the world that we were number one. The World Cup loss became a distant memory as we celebrated on the field, relishing what had been one of our best tournaments ever. We'd outscored our opponents 38–0, never once letting a ball into our goal. We were joyful and proud, and we were headed to the Olympics.

Never Let Up

The final game of the CONCACAF Olympic qualifying tournament didn't mean much in the scheme of things. We were already granted entry into Olympics, so we didn't have to win. But you should never slack off on your goals just because something big isn't on the line. Work hard for the sake of showing yourself and the world how successful you can be. In Abby's case, she broke records in a game that didn't even really mean much! Put your all into everything you do because if you perform below your abilities, you're cheating yourself.

CHAPTER 37

We had six months to wait before the Olympics, but we weren't going to be just sitting around. We had the Algarve Cup in Portugal ahead of us, a few friendly matches, and a tournament in Sweden before the flight to London. I was living out of a suitcase, but I loved it!

Pia would also be naming the eighteen-person roster in late May. I knew there was a chance I wouldn't be on it, but after playing so well at the qualifying tournament, the likelihood was slim.

The Algarve Cup in late February and early March wound up being like a rehearsal for the Olympics. Most of the teams we'd face in London were there, and they were all playing their best. Even though we didn't win the tournament—we were defeated by Japan in the semifinals and came in third place—I felt like I'd grown by leaps and bounds as a player and as a contributor to the team. And in the third-place match against Sweden, I scored my first hat trick on the national squad!

Canada ended up winning the whole tournament, defeating Japan. With that, the outlook for the Olympics became clearer and clearer for us. Japan and Canada were the teams to watch out for. We'd played each many times, and in the case of Canada's Christine Sinclair, I'd played *with* her on the Flash. Team Canada were going to be tough opponents in London. We'd have to keep practicing with that in mind.

But if the Algarve Cup was a rehearsal, the Sweden Invitational in June was a dress rehearsal. The tournament featured only three teams—us, Japan, and Sweden—who were the three top finishers from 2011's World Cup. Pia promised us that Sweden in the summer would be glorious, and it was. The games were right before the summer solstice, so the sun hung in the sky until midnight, and the weather couldn't have been more pleasant.

We played beautifully, beating Sweden 3–1 and Japan 4–1. I started in both games and scored three goals between them, and with a total of seventeen goals for the season, I became the team's scoring leader.

When the roster for the Olympics was named, I was on it. I'd worked so hard for it, and I'd made it. My dream of wearing Olympic gold was feeling more real by the day.

As we boarded the plane for London at the beginning of July, we were excited, nervous, thrilled, confident, happy, and in disbelief all at the same time. *This was the Olympics*. We'd been training for this for almost a year, and we were ready. It was sure to be a grand event, but we couldn't have known it would be the biggest moment of our lives.

Prepare and Practice

Preparation is everything when you're going after your goals. The Olympics were my single biggest dream— they were something I'd been thinking about since I was a kid. And after the World Cup loss, we wanted the gold medal more than anything. But we wouldn't have felt as ready as we did if we hadn't practiced every day, twice a day. You will get nowhere without practice, so put your heart into it every single day. I promise it will pay off!

eing at the Olympics was surreal. We were set to play in stadiums that were steeped in history, where some of the most exciting soccer games had been played. The English soccer leagues are hugely popular, so much so that they're followed internationally, and you can turn on your television on Saturday morning in the United States and see Manchester United or Arsenal or Liverpool playing. We knew that in addition to the fact that it was *the Olympics*, the country's passion for the game would bring out the crowds. But I never expected the energy to be as great as it was.

We missed the opening ceremonies because we were already playing matches, so we didn't get to walk along with the American contingent, carrying the flag and smiling and waving for the cameras. Instead, we held our own opening ceremony. We dressed up in the outfits the US Olympic Committee had provided, and we marched and paraded around the hotel and our dining room. We posted some pictures on social media, then went back upstairs and rested up for our game the next day.

There were twelve teams there—eleven who'd qualified, and England, who was given entry because they were the host country. As with other tournaments, we'd compete in the group stage first, where we'd play three games, with group winners, runners-up, and the two best third-ranked teams advancing to the quarterfinals. That was when the knockout stage started—if you lost in the quarterfinals, you were out.

We got off to a rocky start in our first game against France. In the first fifteen minutes, France scored twice, and we were shocked. Then Shannon Boxx, our center midfielder, went down with a hamstring injury. We were down 2–0 and had to make an early substitution. Could this get worse? While a loss in the group stage wouldn't mean elimination, it certainly wasn't the way we wanted to begin things. But we knew that if we stayed calm and played our hardest, things would take a turn for the better.

Abby and I had forged such a bond by this point, and soon after the second goal, we looked at each other and said, "All right, a goal each." As Hope said later, we were ice-cold and we knew we could do it. And sure enough, Abby and I each scored by the half.

We fought back more in the second half and went on to win 4–2, with me scoring the last goal of the game. We were relieved, thrilled, and determined not to go down 2–0 again!

Our second game in the group stage was three days later against Colombia, and boy, was it dramatic. Soccer is not always the most ethical sport. While it doesn't happen as often in the United States, players often flop on the field to fake a foul and get a penalty kick, or people trip other players, trying to make it look like an accident. Penalties exist to punish and prevent this kind of behavior.

We were up 1–0 in the first half, and in the thirty-ninth minute Abby was running toward the goal to get in position. Right then, one of the Colombian players sucker punched her right in the eye. You read that right—she hit her in the face! Abby went down, writhing in pain.

I couldn't believe it. There Abby was on the ground, kicking the turf, and I could only imagine what was going through her head.

Abby later said about the incident, "You think about yourself and what you would do on the street if somebody were to sucker punch you. And you have all of the lists of things that you would probably do to retaliate, but this is Olympics, and I can't risk getting a red card. I can't risk getting a yellow card."

So Abby took action the best way she knew how. Despite getting taunted and then hit in the neck by the same player in the second half, Abby scored a goal in the seventy-fourth minute, capturing the record for the most goals in the Olympics. Her celebration was hilarious. After she scored, she went up to the cameras and used her fingers to open her bruised and swollen eye. It was the perfect retaliation.

Then we scored one more goal and beat Colombia 3–0.

After our victory against Colombia, Brandi Chastain made a comment on ESPN about our defense. She said that we'd played an A-minus game mostly because of defensive issues, and she called out Rachel Buehler.

This really rubbed Hope the wrong way, and she took to Twitter. She wrote:

Lay off commentating about defending and [goalkeeping] until you get more educated @brandichastain the game has changed from a decade ago.

Hope's known to be outspoken, so no one on our team was surprised or upset. And if you'll recall, I know a thing or two about Twitter outbursts, so I won't judge her. But the press had been critical of Hope, and that brought the mood of the whole team down. We were on a winning streak, and suddenly, people were talking about everything *but* how we were playing.

Abby decided that in our next game, which was against North Korea, that was going to change. She just wanted people to forget what had happened. Plus, the game was on Hope's birthday, so we thought she needed some fun. Abby proposed that Hope would do the worm if anyone on our team scored. No one thought Hope would agree—she usually didn't join in celebrations—but she did!

With the possibility of a worm-dancing goalkeeper in our future, the mood was light when we hit the field at Old Trafford, the historic stadium where Manchester United plays. North Korea was a formidable opponent, but we just played better, and Abby scored in the twenty-fifth minute. Sure enough, Hope dropped to the ground and did the worm! Christie Rampone joined in, and we all grabbed hands and did a little worm wave with our arms. It was hilarious, and it brought us all together in the same way making those snow angels had done years before. In any stressful situation, it's so important to laugh.

Then we went on to win 1–0!

Laughter Is the Best Medicine

There was so much stress at the beginning of the Olympics, but laughter took us through it. If Abby hadn't persuaded Hope to do the worm, her battle with

Brandi Chastain might have left a bad taste in people's mouths. But by laughing and having fun, we showed ourselves and the world that we could move on. Lightening the mood—by telling a joke, watching a funny movie, or doing something silly—can help lessen yours and other people's tension. Laughter really is the best medicine.

CHAPTER 39

P ia said something after our next match—the quarterfinal game against New Zealand—that I think can really help you as you're working toward making your dreams come true. If you're succeeding and climbing higher and higher, you're going to feel a great drive to win. It almost becomes an expectation. And, in fact, you may thrive on it. About us, Pia said, "It's a winning team, so they've been living with the pressure. I just look at the team and it feels like they perform under pressure. They like the pressure. The harder it is, the more you get out of the team."

You have to embrace the stress that's put upon you and that you put upon yourself. Let it drive you ahead. It's like the adrenaline you feel if something scary happens—it causes you to run faster than you've ever run. And that's what we were feeling as we headed into the stadium to play New Zealand. If we lost this game, we were out of the Olympics. That was just *not* going to happen.

We were so pumped up as we headed onto the field,

and we didn't let up the entire game. Abby scored first, in the twenty-seventh minute, off an assist from me. I had a lot of chances for goals—one shot early on and a later pass from Megan that went right past me as I slid for it—but I didn't get any in. And that was okay. As long as the team won, I was happy.

A 1–0 lead is good, but it's not a slam dunk, so we headed into the second half determined to make our lead decisive. It was an aggressive game, and I got knocked to the ground so hard that the opposing player and I had to be checked out by a medic on the field, but we both picked ourselves up and kept playing. You might have seen this on YouTube—it went viral for a day or two.

With ten minutes left in the game, my good friend Sydney Leroux, who was at that point the youngest player on the team, came onto the field to replace me. I had known Sydney so long and wanted to see her have her moment. Sure enough, she was dominant, and when Tobin made a long pass down the field, Sydney captured it, gained control, and took off. She kicked it hard . . . right through the goalie's legs.

The look on Sydney's face after she scored, putting us up 2–0, was one of utter disbelief and sheer exhilaration. I jumped off the bench and ran onto the field to congratulate her. This was her first Olympic goal, and it had sealed our victory in that game. Pia had used Sydney to change the energy of the game, as she'd done so many times with me, and it had worked. We had won.

We went into the locker room euphoric but tired. It had been a long day, but we vowed to stay charged up. We had a big game ahead of us—the semifinal against Canada. Canada had won the Algarve Cup, so we thought the game might not be easy. But we had no idea just how difficult it would be. . . .

Celebrate Others' Successes

Feeling happy for other people when they make their goals can be just as exciting as when you make your own. When Sydney subbed for me, of course I was disappointed not to be playing, but I was happy for her. And then she scored! I think seeing that look on her face was one of the happiest moments of the Olympics for me. My friend hit a huge milestone and propelled us all forward. You may feel jealous when someone else does well, and while that's natural, it doesn't help you. If anything, it's counterproductive. You may begin comparing yourself to another person when instead you should be working to the best of your abilities. Try to be happy for other people when they do well—you'd want the same from them.

CHAPTER 40

August 6, 2012, was a typical English night: a little damp, with just a slight chill in the air. As I wrapped my jacket around my shoulders and headed into Old Trafford with my teammates, I had no inkling how significant the night ahead would be. I just knew I had to focus on one thing: winning.

If the USA beat Canada, we'd move on to the Olympic final and play Japan. My teammates and I were prepared to do whatever we had to do to get to that final, gold-medal game. We just *had* to have the opportunity to show the world that last year's World Cup loss to Japan was a fluke. *We* were the best team in the world, not them. So Canada was just going to be a bump in the road. In fact, they were the lowest ranked of all the semi-final teams, so while they were good, we knew we were better. We'd just power through this game like we had all the others—by working as a team, being aggressive, and fending off the defenders to score some goals.

There were more than twenty-six thousand people in

the stands that night at the "Theatre of Dreams." That's the nickname for Old Trafford, the stadium where David Beckham had played and where some of the fiercest rivalries in English soccer had unfolded. I could hear the chants of "USA! USA!" as the starting whistle was blown.

We kicked off, with me passing the ball back to Lauren Cheney. Within ten seconds Lauren was tripped, signifying the kind of game that was ahead of us. Canada was obviously hungry. Lauren took a great free kick from midfield, but the Canadians got to the ball before we could, quickly getting the ball out of the box.

But then it was my turn. I dribbled the ball past some defenders, my eye on Abby, ready to pass to her in the midfield. But before I could, a defender hit me on my right shoulder and knocked me off my feet. We were only a minute into the game, and I'd already been fouled. Canada was playing aggressively, and we'd have to be aggressive back.

Carli Lloyd took the free kick, but the ball whizzed past Megan Rapinoe, who was in the box and might have had a winning shot if she'd been able to get to the ball sooner.

The next ten minutes or so passed quickly. We did a great job of keeping the ball away from Hope, and I imagined she was even kind of bored as we kept the ball in the midfield, passing from player to player. Megan made a powerful shot early on, but the Canadian goalie deflected it.

Nineteen minutes in, I think we were all ready for some action. Canadian player Melissa Tancredi took the ball down the field toward our goal. Megan tried to fend her off with her left arm, and sure enough, Tancredi went down. The Canadians were going to get a free kick. It was a long kick, and we were just too much of a swarm. We quickly shot the ball back toward the sideline. Things were getting a little heated, and as one announcer said, the Canadian team had stopped "easing into the match." They were all in.

Sure enough, the aggressiveness they'd shown in the first minute of play returned about twenty-one minutes in. They took the ball down the field toward Hope, and after a short pass, Melissa Tancredi tapped the ball over to Christine Sinclair, who kicked it right in. It was an easy goal for them, and it was the best play of the game so far. We'd been so feisty and played so hard for the bulk of the half, and yet Canada had struck first. It stung.

I didn't know it then, but with that goal, Christine Sinclair marked her 141st national goal, only one behind Abby's record.

About a half hour into the game, Abby collided with Melissa Tancredi, and we got a free kick. It sailed long and high . . . and right at me. Now, headers are not my strong suit. That's Abby all the way. She's the one with three

Twitter fan accounts devoted just to her head (seriously, check them out at @WambachHead, @WambachsHead and @AbbyWambachHead) and a Facebook fan page where her head is always making fun of her feet. Pia is always saying that headers are my weakness, so when I jumped in the air, made contact, and the ball glanced just to the left of the goal, I guess I wasn't surprised.

When the halftime whistle blew at forty-five minutes, Canada was still up 1–0. We'd made some great plays, but we hadn't scored, even though we'd had the ball 55 percent of the time. Canada had taken two shots, and one had gone in.

But we'd be back. We were going to win this game. Just like when my sisters used to think there was no way I could beat them at Monopoly or cards, I always knew I could and I would. We were just waiting for the right moment.

Stay Confident

Confidence is so important as you try to reach your goals. Try to never doubt yourself—it doesn't do you any good. When we went into the locker room during halftime, we were down, but we weren't going to let it *get* us down. We were pumped—there were still at least forty-five minutes to even things out. Remain confident even when you're not ahead. Don't worry. You'll get there!

CHAPTER 41

We went back to the field more eager to win than ever, and pretty soon the game got physical. At one point Abby was knocked to the ground in a chase after the ball, and the other player's cleats dug into her right leg. (If you've never had studs scrape into your leg at high speed, consider yourself lucky.) Then about a minute later, Abby jumped for the ball in the box, and she got sandwiched between two Canadian players. She was really taking a beating!

And then in the fifty-fourth minute the craziest thing happened. Megan Rapinoe was taking a corner kick, and we were all cramped around the box, the Canadians ready to hustle the ball away from the goal and us determined to get it in. Megan kicked hard. The ball sailed through the air, fast, just over one Canadian player's head, and after a slight arch, it landed perfectly right inside in the near corner of the goal. I saw a pile of white Canadian jerseys fall into the goal after it, and I instantly knew what had happened. GOAL!

Initially we couldn't figure out exactly how the ball had gone in. Had the Canadian goalie's knee glanced it? Had Christine Sinclair mistakenly knocked it in? No. It was that rare, awe-inspiring thing called the Olympic goal. That's a point scored off a corner kick in which no one touches it—the ball just sails in. It could be caused by the wind, a great spin on the ball, or just dumb luck, but it's a beautiful thing.

As Megan jumped into my arms and hugged me tight, I didn't think I'd ever been so happy. We were back in the game, tied 1–1.

For the next ten minutes, though, the chants of "Let's Go Canada" sounded a little louder than they had earlier in the game. When you stop being the underdog, sometimes people stop rooting for you. Don't let that stop you! The will to win is inside yourself—it doesn't come from outside. Canada must have been motivated by the cheers, though, because as the sixty-sixth minute ticked by, they got aggressive. Tancredi made a perfect cross from the left side of the field, into our box, and right to the head of Christine Sinclair. She knocked the ball in, just like that. And with that header—Abby's signature move—she tied my dear friend's international goal record. Canada went up 2–1.

We shot back quickly. We had to. As one announcer said, when we're in a mood, nothing can stop us. We were so fired up as we took the ball down the field in the sixty-ninth minute of play, and when a long pass landed right at Megan's feet, she belted the ball from seventy feet. That's a *long* kick, but that's one of the things Megan's best at! It was amazing—the ball ripped through the air, hit the goalpost, and went right in. Megan scored again! We were now tied 2–2.

Throughout the years I've learned *never* to lose my competitive edge. I'm the most competitive person I know, and it always pushes me a little further. So I remember thinking we had to go into overdrive after Megan's goal. A tie was good, but we had to get ahead. Apparently Canada felt the same, though, because just a few minutes later Christine Sinclair scored another goal for Canada, heading the ball into the goal off a corner kick. There was nothing Hope could have done to stop it. It was now 3–2 Canada, and Christine Sinclair had overtaken Abby's international scoring record and gained ground on Mia Hamm's record. And we were still behind, with elimination from the Olympics on the line.

We couldn't lose. We just couldn't. We had to either play harder and better or catch a break. And as the seventy-eighth minute of play began, the latter happened.

I think one of the hardest jobs in the world is being a soccer referee. They're all alone on the field, running three to five miles each game. They have to be in the best shape of their life, maybe even better than the players. I can get a sub—the referee can't. And every single call on the field is up to them.

The referee in our game, Christiana Pedersen, took a lot of heat for what happened in the seventy-eighth minute. Megan had just taken a corner kick that the Canadian goalie, Erin McLeod, had caught. There's a rule in soccer called the six-second penalty, which means that the goalie can't hold on to the ball for more than six seconds before kicking it away. This call is rarely enforced—most refs take it for granted that the goalie wants to get the ball back into play, so they just let the rule slide. But that doesn't mean that the players aren't paying attention. Abby was near Christiana Pedersen, counting the seconds tick by. In fact, she'd been counting all game since the Canadian keeper was taking at least twelve seconds every time she had the ball. *Five . . . six . . . seven . . .* until Abby hit ten. This time, Pedersen blew the whistle.

Megan got to take a penalty kick from the spot of the violation—*way* inside the penalty area. The Canadians were lined up like soldiers, six white jerseys right in a line when Megan kicked—and the ball hit two Canadians right in the hands and arms. Although players instinctively try to protect themselves when a ball is coming toward them, if your arm isn't in a natural position when the ball hits you, it's considered a handball. That's what Pedersen saw, and she called the violation. Boy, did that anger the Canadian coach and players. They didn't believe it was a handball.

So it was Abby against McLeod, and the decks were stacked against McLeod. Not only was she reeling from two sudden, controversial calls, but she was about to face one of the world's most successful close-range kickers, and she had to do it alone.

Abby paused. She shot, and she nailed it, BOOM, right into the goal.

We were tied 3–3 with just over ten minutes left in regulation. But ten minutes can be a lifetime in a soccer game.

Life Can Be Unfair

In any kind of competition, or in the pursuit of any kind of goal, things may happen that you consider flat-out wrong. A teacher may give you an undeserved C on a paper, or a controversial call in a game might happen. But you have to push ahead. If the Canadians had pitched a fit about the handball call, it would have disrupted things even further, and players might have been ejected from the game. But instead they simply filed complaints with the Olympic committee, which was the appropriate course of action. Don't dwell on why unfair things happen because you can't change the past—just try your best to deal with it calmly.

CHAPTER 42

At the end of regulation we were still tied 3–3. We'd had one chance to get a goal: I'd taken the ball down the field against one defender and passed it to Abby, but she kicked it just wide. When she fell to the ground and slapped her hands against her head, I knew she was frustrated. So was I.

The rules in the Olympics are much like other tournaments—if you're tied after ninety minutes, you have two periods of extra time, each fifteen minutes long. Hopefully someone will have won by the end of those, but if they haven't, you go into a penalty shoot-out. And believe it or not, there has never, ever been a shoot-out in Olympic women's soccer.

Extra time started, and we were off to the races. Both teams were playing hard and playing fast, and I could see all my teammates breathing heavily as we ran up and back down the field. Sydney Leroux took a shot early on, and later Abby almost got one in off her world-famous head, but it wasn't to be.

I had been playing hard for almost two hours when the first period of extra time came to a close. We were all exhausted. It had been 105 minutes, and we were playing one of the most high-pressure games of our lives! When we stood in the huddle, awaiting the beginning of the final fifteen minutes of play, Abby, not Pia, was the one doing all the talking. We never get much time between breaks in play, so she spoke fast.

"Everybody needs to believe in each other right now. And keep it together. *Believe* we're going to win. We're going to do it if we play as a team. We can do this!"

Abby is always so motivating, especially at critical moments. And here she was, psyching us up in a way she never had before.

When we started again, it was like unarmed combat, as one announcer said. Players were going down left and right and staying down much longer than they would have at the beginning of the game. That's what happens when you've played for that long: Everything just hurts worse. You cramp up, old injuries come back to haunt you, and if you haven't had enough water, your sides will start splitting. I was knocked down right outside the Canadian goal line at about the 113th minute—Abby thought it was a penalty, but sadly, it wasn't—and I had to lie there just to catch my breath. *Get up, Alex. . . . Get up and win this game once and for all.*

About 117 minutes in, the Canadians were desperately defending against two plays that could have been shots on goal. And then, with two minutes before the end of extra time, I made a beautiful pass right to Abby, who was waiting in the penalty box. She jumped, the ball sailed perfectly off the side of her head . . . and it soared into the air, touching the tips of the Canadian goalkeeper's fingers and bouncing off the top bar of the goal without going in. Another missed goal. Another chance to end the game lost.

Even though we were still tied, I could just feel that the game was all ours. We'd been at the goal twice as much as Canada, and we'd taken several amazing shots in just a few minutes. At 120 minutes they added three minutes of stoppage time, and I remember feeling my best.

Now, I didn't know this at the time, but everybody was already talking about what it was going to be like when regulation time ended and we had to take penalty kicks. They just expected that the end of this game would be exactly like the World Cup final against Japan. But I was determined it wouldn't be.

And sure enough, with forty-five seconds left in the game—forty-five seconds before the first penalty shoot-out in Olympic women's history—Heather O'Reilly ran harder than I've ever seen her run toward a ball that was about to go out of bounds to the right of the Canadian goal. She caught it and kicked it hard, crossing it perfectly toward the goal. And there I was, standing in a swarm of white jerseys. I told myself, *C'mon, Alex. All you have to do is get your head on the ball. Connect.* I jumped and felt the ball against my head, the part of my body that had been such a disappointment to me in so many games.

And then I heard a roar from the crowd that rivaled any cheering I'd ever heard. It was as if every person in the Theatre of Dreams had stood up, on cue, and screamed at the top of their lungs. And I knew it. *The ball had gone in. I'd done it. We'd won the game.*

As my teammates hugged me, I noticed tears welling up in my eyes. "I love you," I heard Abby say to me. "I think I'm in love with you in this moment because you just sent us to the gold-medal game." The tears burst from my eyes.

We still had a few seconds left to play, so we finished out the game, and then I let myself relax. I cried on the field—*who does that?*—but it felt good. I knew my parents were up there crying too, and I knew they were proud.

We were going to the finals.

Know Your Weaknesses

Your weaknesses may not always let you down. You may be terrible at math and feel incredibly nervous before a geometry test, but you just might surprise yourself and get a good grade. Somehow you just knew the answers, or you worked out how to figure them out. Look at my headers—I'd never done them well. But I practiced, and a header took us into the gold-medal Olympic game. Know your weaknesses and work at them despite your fear.

CHAPTER 43

It had been one year and twenty-three days since Japan had beaten us in the World Cup. And every single one of those days had filled me with a drive to win unlike any I'd felt before.

Three days after the semifinal win, it was hard not to still feel happy. Some people had called my match-winning goal "Morgan's Miracle," but I knew it was no miracle—that moment was what I'd been training for my whole life. And it had all brought me here, to Wembley Stadium, the second-largest stadium in all of Europe and the most expensive stadium in the world. As we walked onto the field in front of eighty thousand people, the noise was deafening. Just a few years before, a women's soccer team wouldn't have been able to fill a stadium that large, but we'd proven ourselves year after year, and the crowds had responded. Now here we were about to face an epic rematch against Japan, and both teams were determined to win.

We wanted to taste victory, and Japan wanted to show the world that their first Olympic final appearance was no fluke.

When the starting whistle blew, we acted fast, and I was all over the field within minutes. Three minutes in I took a shot on the goal, but it landed squarely in the goalie's hands. *Next time!*

And next time came less than five minutes later. We were all crowded close to the Japanese penalty box after a breathless run toward the goal. Tobin kicked the ball over from the left side of the field, and then I turned it around, cutting it back toward Abby, who was waiting near the goal box. But Carli Lloyd was on her way toward it, too, and she just nodded it right into the goal, like there was some sort of invisible force coming right out of her head into the ball. The ball sailed right into the net like it was shot out of a gun.

I could tell how frustrated the Japanese players were. They were already at a disadvantage in terms of their size. We're a tall bunch of girls. Abby is five-eleven, and I'm pretty tall at five-eight. But one of their players is five feet and one half inch. Her head barely comes up to Abby's neck! So when the Japanese players began advancing toward us about seventeen minutes in, I knew it was because of their technical genius—they were disciplined and liked to press hard. They took some frightening shots on goal, and a kick by their forward Yūki Ōgimi made Hope jump so high in the air that when she fell, it looked like a tree getting blown over and landing with a *thud* on the ground.

I imagine they grew even more frustrated when one of their players almost headed the ball into her own goal at around twenty-seven minutes. We had just taken a long shot from way outside the penalty area—there's almost no chance it could have gone in—but one of their defenders hit it the wrong way, and lucky for her the goalpost deflected it. I was right there and saw it all unfold. If it had gone in, it would have been humiliating. Especially in the Olympic final!

As the waning seconds of the first half came and went, we were up 1–0. We marched into the locker room excited but nervous. This game was so close, and we needed to double our efforts to secure a victory.

I don't think any of us headed into the second half thinking we were guaranteed a win. We knew how strong Japan could be, but most of all, we remembered last year. The sting of the World Cup loss was still all too real. Even though the US women's team had won Olympic gold four years ago at Beijing, this game felt like the most important of our lives. And, of course, this was my first Olympic final. I'd only gotten to watch the Beijing games on TV!

When the whistle blew, the Japanese came on strong, knocking Hope to the ground after an aggressive shot right at the goal line. But pretty quickly after that, the game was ours again. I was a lot fiercer this half—I had the ball more, and I took it down the field confidently. I was starting to feel good. . . . Maybe we really would take home the gold.

At about fifty-three minutes in, that possibility became even more likely. Megan secured the ball and passed it to Carli Lloyd well back into the midfield. Carli dribbled it toward the Japanese goal all on her own, and I could see her getting closer and closer to the penalty box. I was far to her left, wide open, and Abby was to her right. Would she pass it to one of us?

Here's the beautiful thing about soccer. It's a team sport, and you trust your teammates 100 percent. You have to. In that moment I believed in what Carli was doing, and I had faith that if she needed to pass to me or to Abby, she would. We were there for her, and we could take a shot if we had to. But I trusted she knew what to do.

It turned out, she didn't need to lean on me or Abby. From behind the penalty line, she kicked hard, and the ball went right into the left corner of the net. A long, clean, beautiful goal. We were up 2–0!

Coming back from two behind with thirty-five minutes left in the game wasn't an easy prospect for

Japan. Time wasn't on their side, and chances were they wouldn't be able to score quickly given the way they'd been playing. We had been taking the ball away from them too much, even though they seemed to have possession more than we did.

But they made a valiant effort. In the sixty-third minute of play, the Japanese players passed the ball back and forth for what seemed like forever, then kicked it left to one of their star players, Shinobu Ohno, who was in the penalty box. Ohno tapped it over to Homare Sawa, who kicked it past Hope and almost in. We defended it, but Sawa got it again and passed it to Yūki Ōgimi, who was waiting for it only a few feet from the goal. She shot it right in. The score was 2–1.

The memory of Japan coming back from behind— twice—in the World Cup was fresh in my mind. They'd done this before. Could they do it again? I determined right then and there that wasn't going to happen.

In the stands, Pia was on her feet, looking a little more anxious than normal. She knew what the Japanese team was capable of—they could be relentless!

I got the ball in the seventy-fourth minute and took it down the field, fast. As I got closer to the goal, I realized I had to make a decision: take a shot or pass it to Abby. I decided to take the shot, which went long and high and nowhere near the goal.

We are faced with a million decisions in a ninety-minute soccer match. Do we pass? Do we run? Or do we shoot? In that scenario, I made the wrong choice. I should have passed to Abby. But I refused to dwell on it. Some decisions have bigger consequences than others, and you just have to accept that. And sometimes something that seems right to you will seem wrong to someone else. You just have to trust your gut when faced with a difficult choice and try not to regret whatever follows next.

In the eighty-second minute Hope Solo made one of the most spectacular saves I've ever seen. Mana Iwabuchi stole the ball from Christie Rampone and came up on Hope fast. They were staring at each other in a standoff, but then Mana charged, kicking the ball toward the back post. But Hope dove for it, and she made contact with the tips of her fingers. The ball went wide, far away from the goal, and we all breathed a huge sigh of relief. With eight minutes left, we were safe—for now. The press later called it "the save heard 'round the world," and while I can't promise that people who were watching on TV felt the impact of Hope's amazing play, I can tell you that standing on the field that night, I did.

The chants of "USA! USA!" grew louder and louder as the final minutes of the game ticked away. At the end of ninety minutes of regulation, we had two minutes of stoppage time. *Two minutes to gold. Two minutes to glory*, I kept telling myself. Winning a gold medal at the Olympics had been my dream for as long as I could remember, and it was so close I could taste it.

I could tell the Japanese players weren't ready to give up, but when the final whistle blew, it was over, and the gold was ours. We all ran to the middle of the field and held one another so tightly I thought I might get crushed.

At one point in the midst of our celebrations I looked over and saw the Japanese team standing in a huddle. Almost all of them were crying. I don't know if it was out of exhaustion, out of sadness, or out of a combination of both, but I didn't blame them. It had been an emotional game. They had played so beautifully and so technically, and I felt honored for having had the opportunity to be on the field with them. Redemption felt great, but we had sympathy for their loss, too.

Still, I was smiling ear to ear for the next half hour. I looked over at one point and saw Megan crying—she looked so happy, but tears were streaming down her face. Maybe she was feeling relief. With our win, all the tension we'd felt for weeks had flown out the window.

Soon the medal ceremony began, and the Canadian team came back onto the field to claim their bronze medals. They had beaten France in a fantastic match, and I was happy to see them rewarded for their fine play.

After they were honored, it was Japan's turn. And then it was ours.

As the American flag rose in the air just above the Canadian and Japanese flags, we all smiled wide and sang along to the national anthem together, positively glowing. We held one another, and I looked down and saw the shining gold medal around my neck.

This was, without a doubt, the greatest achievement of my life.

Be a Good Winner

You just accomplished a goal—congratulations! But a person you're close to might not have. Your friend sitting next to you in history class may have gotten a C when you got an A. Don't gloat—it will only make others resent you. When we won Olympic gold, we celebrated, but we also shook the Japanese players' hands immediately and congratulated them on playing so well. Good sportsmanship creates good energy in any situation.

CHAPTER 44

It's so important to take time to reflect and celebrate when you achieve something. Don't just move on— really soak in the moment and take pride in what you've done. You may be caught up in a whirlwind, but don't let that stop you from really *feeling* it. That's what we did after the Olympics. There were interviews all over the place: national TV, radio shows, and of course, there were the closing ceremonies.

But for me, the most fun was celebrating with my family. The night after the final, we partied like it was ten New Year's Eves all wrapped into one. My parents dropped me off at the Olympic Village at 6:30 a.m., took the Tube (the London subway) back to their hotel, and fell asleep on the train! They ended up at the end of the subway line and couldn't get back to their hotel till 10:00 a.m. Dad missed his flight home! It was expensive to rebook his flight, of course, but we were too hopped up on our win to be upset. We thought it was absolutely hysterical.

The interviews gave us time to think about the past few weeks. Wearing a gold medal was the biggest victory in my life, and honestly, it was surreal. But getting to talk about it helped it sink in. And as I realized what had happened, I felt so grateful. I had wonderful parents, the best boyfriend in the world, a team I loved, and I'd made my dreams come true. While there was still so much to do, I wanted to take the time to bask in it.

And I did. Going home to Seattle put routine and consistency back into my life, and that gave me a chance to stop, reflect, and just feel happy. Then the national team crossed the United States in a ten-game celebration tour, playing against other countries. It was a lot of work, but so much fun now that the pressure was off.

After the most intense summer of my life, I was starting to feel my heart and my body return to where they needed to be—in balance.

A big part of keeping yourself in balance and harmony is staying fit. Even when I'm not on the field, exercise is part of living well for me.

I've talked a lot about my soccer training in this book—injury prevention, the time I devote to practice, and the mental preparation needed for the game—but my soccer training may not be perfectly suited to you. No matter what you do, it's important to stay healthy.

That will help you find the balance that's key to living better. Taking care of yourself is crucial to getting what you want in life, and exercise and good eating are the main components of that.

I always say that if you're not sweating, you're not working hard enough. You should always break a sweat when you exercise. It means your heart is pumping, and that means you're improving your cardiovascular health. Stretching is key, too, and yoga can help with that. I love yoga so much. It restores my mind, keeps me in balance (mentally and physically), and helps build tone. Try to exercise three to four times a week for about a half hour, and please don't feel that you have to be a member of a gym to get fit! Some easy ways to get exercise include swimming, walking on the beach, walking fast anywhere (your neighborhood or around a track), jogging, or biking. It doesn't matter—just get your heart pumping.

Don't discount strength training, too. It's as important as cardiovascular health. You don't need to buy anything like weights or machines. Sometimes all you need is a little floor space and some things you should see around the gym: ropes, medicine balls, a BOSU ball, a Physioball, and some dumbbells relative to your weight. I don't even use the big gym equipment myself.

It's always good to surprise your body, too, so

alternate your routines. You don't want your body to get used to certain exercises or else you won't get the maximum results. I always switch up my workouts, never just running at one pace or doing the same gym routine and number of push-ups or dumbbell exercises.

Eating well is key to good health too. Drink lots and lots of water—eight eight-ounce cups a day at a minimum—and stay away from processed foods like chips and cookies. Eat fruits, vegetables, lean meats, and healthy snacks like nuts. We all have foods we love that may not be so healthy for you—mine is Mexican food, which can be loaded with sour cream and cheese—but try to emphasize the healthy option in whatever that food is. For example, I can load up a taco with salsa and guacamole. Those are nutritious choices!

Making healthy choices requires discipline, but if you stick to it, you're going to have more energy, mental clarity, feel happier, and look better. How much exercise you choose to do and how nutritious your diet is is ultimately your choice, but believe me, no one ever regrets a hard workout or a delicious, nutritious meal. If you feel stronger and better, you're going to have more energy to make goals and go after them, and you're going to find it easier and more fun to work harder. I feel refreshed and focused after doing yoga, and it makes my whole day better. Try to make a healthy change today—drop the doughnut and pick up an apple, or go for a walk instead of watching TV—and see how you feel. I promise you won't regret it.

Do What's Best for You

The recommendations I've made above may not be right for you. If you've never exercised before, you may be terrified by the idea of working out with an exercise ball, and that's okay. Start small and do whatever you can, as long as it's good for your health. Don't expect that you can develop nutritious eating habits in a day—it might take weeks or years. Be realistic, set your own timelines, and just focus on the goal of making healthy choices every day.

CHAPTER 45

The year 2012 had been the most exciting one of my life. I was so grateful for everything that had been given to me and that I'd worked for, and I didn't take any of it for granted. When something wonderful happens to you—from a good grade to a great year—don't forget to stop and be thankful. It's what you've worked for, after all!

I didn't think it could get any better, but it did. At the end of the year I was named US Soccer's 2012 Female Athlete of the Year, a prize that had been voted on by fans, the media, and soccer representatives. It was such an honor, especially because of the fans. I had started to get a fan base at games, and I loved meeting every single person who was there for me. My dad once told me I should always be the last person signing autographs, and I am (most of the time!). I remember being a little girl scrambling for an autograph after a game, so I know how fans feel. Plus, if I can inspire anyone to chase after their dreams, I'll do it.

As 2013 arrived, I knew there was still so much to do. And high on my list of priorities was helping to see women's soccer in the United States gain the respect it deserved. Thankfully, the formation of a new league was going to help with that.

The National Women's Soccer League had been in the works for only a year—roundtable discussions about it had started after the WPS folded. Funding for it was being provided by the US, Canadian, and Mexican soccer foundations, who were all heavily invested. They wanted to see female soccer players have a world-class league to play in. They settled on having eight teams, and they decided to divide the national team players among the squads in an allocation process so that each squad would be evenly balanced.

I wanted so much for this league to work. It's still a mystery to me why women's soccer has had trouble gaining ground in the United States—we're the best players in the world! But I suppose it's all part of the problem that women's sports in general face. There's just not enough money, and for whatever reason, sports are historically a male domain. I want so much for that to change.

Every player who was going to play in the National Women's Soccer League had to write down three teams they'd like to play for, and then, as I mentioned, a committee would divide us up. I wrote my choices down, and I waited. Finally, in early January it was announced that I would go to the Portland Thorns.

I was thrilled to go to Portland. It's a fantastic sports town and a wonderful place to live, and I knew the community would be supportive. But I was sad to leave Seattle. For the first time in two years, Servando and I had gotten to make a life together, and I was going to have to leave that. Plus, the Sounders had been so gracious to me, especially when national team commitments took me away for most of the year. But you have to prioritize when you're chasing your dreams, and if moving away from my boyfriend meant that I could help start up a new league, I'd do that. We'd made it through separations before, and we'd make it through another. Plus, Seattle and Portland weren't very far away from each other—we could make it work.

The Thorns were going to be a great team. My old teammate Christine Sinclair—who was our nemesis during the Olympic semifinal game—would be my fellow striker, and my national teammates Tobin Heath and Rachel Buehler would be on the Thorns as well. I decided to share an apartment with Allie Long, a former UNC midfielder whom I'd never played with, but whom I knew professionally. Portland was disappointed not to get Megan Rapinoe, who had attended college at the

University of Portland, and Abby Wambach, who made her home there. Megan signed to a team in France, and Abby went to Western New York, much to the thrill of her hometown crowd. Despite not having them, the general consensus was that this was going to be an incredibly powerful squad.

But I had to remember this wasn't just about the US women. Mexico and Canada were paying their respective players' salaries, so this was truly a joint effort among the three countries to get the league going. We had some of Mexico's and Canada's best players on our team—players I'd sparred against in international games—but we were coming together on the Thorns. We were so excited.

The start of something new is a time of such promise, and you should embrace that excitement. On top of that, the end of something that failed—in this case, the WPS—is always the beginning of a beautiful new thing. Remember, even when something doesn't work on the first or even second try, it might just work on the third. . . .

Keep Trying Even if You Fail

As the saying goes, if at first you don't succeed, try, try again. That was the case with the National Women's Soccer League. The WPS had failed, and the Women's United Soccer Association had folded before it. It would have been easy for people to throw up their hands and say, "Women's soccer just isn't going to work in the United States," but they didn't. They fought, they pooled money, and they realized that fans wanted it. The NWSL is going strong in its second year, and it's expanded by one team with plans for more. You can watch games on ESPN and Fox Sports, which is something that was never an option when I was a kid. So keep trying despite multiple failures— you'll probably succeed sooner rather than later!

CHAPTER 46

If you're really dedicated to something, you might find yourself so busy that you have little time for yourself. I remember running around in high school and college, doing my homework in between practices. I worked on this book when I was rushing to catch a flight *and* while I was in the midst of a tournament! But just remember that you're fitting things in because you're pursuing your passion, so try to keep your eye on the big picture. Try not to let a hectic schedule get you down—it's all a part of chasing your dreams.

I had been living out of a suitcase for the past two years, and the spring of 2013 was no different. I hardly had time to unpack my bags in Portland before I got called up for the Algarve Cup in Portugal. The US national team was still flying high from the Olympics, so being back with the team felt like a celebration. But it was a celebration that was missing one important person, and that was Pia Sundhage.

"I'm going back to Sweden to coach the Swedish

national team," she'd said to the press when she announced the move. "I have long dreamed of becoming Sweden's coach, and now I am so happy."

And she did seem happy. We were a little shocked and pretty upset to lose her, but we couldn't be selfish about it—Sweden was Pia's home, and we knew she'd missed it. She had to follow her dreams as much as we had to follow ours, so we couldn't be angry with her. And it was especially hard not to smile when she started singing Olivia Newton-John's "If Not for You" in an interview, referencing her time with our team. This wasn't the first time she'd sung during an interview, but it was still hilarious.

We decided to send her off in style. Her farewell game was a friendly match against Australia, and we beat them handily, 6–2. After the game, Pia ran a victory lap around the field, hopping and high-stepping, and we serenaded her with "You Are My Sunshine." The fans went crazy. As a good-bye present, we gave her a guitar signed by each of us in a color that couldn't have been more fitting: gold.

Pia had helped balance us, had taken us through some incredible ups and downs, and most of all, had been our friend and our coach. She had basically shaped my career on the national team, taking me off the bench during strategic times and putting me in as a starter at a time the team and I needed it most. I had always been able to be honest with her, and she'd appreciated that. Pia gave me a chance with the team. She believed in me, and for that I'll be forever grateful.

Our new coach was a former Scottish player named Tom Sermanni, who'd coached around the world, most recently in Australia, where he'd led the women's national team to the World Cup quarterfinals in 2007 and 2011. While Pia had been a benevolent dictator, Tom was a little more laid-back. We liked him. He was a good person with tremendous experience under his belt. It was different not having Pia at a major tournament, but we were happy with Tom.

And here we were in Portugal for the Algarve Cup, about to play against Sweden, Pia's team. We had advanced to the semifinals after winning the group stage, and we were literally staring across the sidelines at Pia as we played her team for a chance to go to the finals. It was kind of surreal.

We played hard in the beginning, but Sweden had struck first, going up 1–0 by halftime. If they won, we'd go to the third-place match, and we'd always advanced to the Algarve finals. Doing anything less would be a disappointment. So when the second half started, we were on the attack. In the fifty-sixth minute, Megan made a great corner kick that I got my head on, and the ball went in. We were tied 1–1!

Because we'd won the group stage ahead of Sweden, a tie would take us to the finals, so that was all we needed. And we got it—when the whistle blew, we were still at 1–1. We were off to the finals against Germany.

Germany was ranked #2 in the world, right behind us. But we were confident, despite Megan Rapinoe being pulled off the roster at the last minute because of an injury. My good friend Tobin Heath would replace her in midfield, which would be a little reunion since we played together on the Thorns.

The game was tough, but we played beautifully. I scored in the thirteenth minute and then again in the thirty-third off an assist from Tobin, and we won the game 2–0. We were again Algarve Cup champions—for the ninth time!—and we'd sealed our rank as the #1 soccer team in the world. Under a new coach, this was especially thrilling. We'd shown we could remain strong and stable in the midst of change.

Saying Good-Bye

Sometimes you have to say good-bye to a coach or a mentor who's been instrumental to your goals and dreams. For me, that was Pia. Having her leave the team was devastating, but it was what was best for her—it had nothing to do with us. Try to be strong when you move on from someone you've looked up to and remember that the lessons they taught you are what's most important. What you've learned from them will help you as much or more than their presence. And you'll probably get a different kind of guidance from a new mentor! Try to stay positive—every new person in your life will provide a new learning experience.

CHAPTER 47

A return to the United States after the Algarve Cup meant going back to the Thorns and the beginning of our inaugural season. Our first home game was against the Seattle Reign, and more than sixteen thousand people were in the stands to cheer us on. Can you believe that? That's more people in attendance than any WPS game or any Seattle Sounders game. Walking on the field and seeing that many people there to support us gave me the chills. I thought, *Maybe we're getting there. Maybe a professional soccer league is going to work in the United States.*

People showed up for our away games too. I could hardly believe it—at one point we had seventeen thousand people up in the stands cheering, maybe not entirely for us, but definitely for women's soccer! This was such a promising start.

We did so well that first season, playing in twenty-two games with a 10-6-6 record. I saw almost all of my national teammates at various points on the field, and while they were now my opponents, it was always fun to go against them. Because I'd played with them, I knew so many of their tricks, and playing *against* them always taught me something new.

We were just about to wrap up our season, with only three games left, when I received a nasty wake-up call in the form of a knee injury. Now, I hadn't hurt my knee since my ACL injury when I was seventeen, so when I collided with a Boston Breakers player and felt a sharp pain in my left knee, it was terrifying. I was carried on a stretcher to the locker room for a preliminary evaluation, and after they put a brace on, I went back to the sidelines to watch the rest of the game. A full diagnosis would have to wait.

Thankfully, we found out later it was medial collateral ligament strain—one of the ligaments of the knee—and a few weeks' rest and rehab were going to help me get back on the field. And believe me, I was dying to be out there. The Thorns had qualified for the NWSL championship playoffs, and I thought we had a real chance of winning it. I had to think positive. I wanted to see us win.

I was sidelined during the last few games of the season. But at that point in my career, I knew I had to force myself to be patient when I was injured. At times it killed me not to know my fate, but I rested and did physical therapy, and slowly I got better.

Unfortunately, though, I wasn't well enough to play in our semifinal match against Kansas City. I was healthy enough to be an available substitute, but just not *so* healed that my coaches and I felt comfortable putting me in as a starter. So when I suited up and got ready for the game, it was with the knowledge that I was probably going to be cheering on my colleagues from the sidelines.

But what a game it was. We went down 2–0 early on, which was heartbreaking. But as halftime loomed, Tobin netted a great goal—her first for the Thorns! And we went into the second half 2–1.

Then, in the sixty-fifth minute, we scored another by an assist from Christine Sinclair, and when the whistle blew to signal the end of regulation, we were tied 2–2.

I still hadn't played, and I was itching to get on the field. But sometimes watching someone you love get a goal is as much fun as getting your own, and that's what happened in the 103rd minute, when my roommate, Allie Long, captured the ball and took a shot from eighteen yards. It went in! We'd come back from two down, and if we could make it fifteen more minutes, we were going to the finals.

And we did. The game ended with a 3–2 final score. We were headed to the NWSL championship!

I had thought the semifinal game was exciting, but the championship was nail-biting for a whole new set of reasons.

The Western New York Flash were a tough team. Abby Wambach and Carli Lloyd played for them, so they had the same kind of national team strength that we did. But we had some iffy players going into the game— Tobin was playing through an injury she'd sustained in the semifinals, and I still wasn't 100 percent.

Despite our injuries, the game was incredibly physical and aggressive. There were seventeen fouls in the first half, and Tobin got shoved by a Flash player. Then she got fouled again, which led to a free kick from twenty-five yards back from the goal. She shot, and it was high, long, powerful . . . and right in the goal!

Then early in the second half, our player Kat Williamson fouled Abby Wambach and got a yellow card. Minutes later, she got a red card for taking Abby down just outside the penalty area. Kat was out of the game and we were down to ten players.

I still hadn't gone onto the field, and I was getting antsy. *If I can get a goal, we can seal our win.* But remember, soccer is about teamwork, not about glory. Even if I wasn't playing, we could win.

I finally came on the field in the seventy-first minute, but it didn't change much. We just didn't get to the ball, and the Flash controlled the field. But still, we defended against them. They didn't get any of their shots in.

Then stoppage time came, and I captured the ball off

a throw-in. I passed to Christine Sinclair, who was wide open at the top of the box. We caught them in transition and capitalized on it. She took one touch to set up her right foot and made a perfect, easy shot right past the Flash's goalie. GOAL! Christine had put one away, putting us up 2–0, and soon the whistle blew.

We had done it! In the championship game of the inaugural NWSL season, we had won. I was so proud, not just for us, but for women's soccer in general. What a thrilling end to a beautiful year.

Thank Your Supporters

I couldn't believe how many people showed up to cheer on the NWSL teams that first season. People *loved* watching us, and fans waited at the end of the game for us to sign autographs. I appreciate the support of each and every one of my fans, and their encouragement pushes me to be a better player. I grant every autograph request and answer all of my mail, thanking all my fans for their support. If you win a speech team tournament or win an award, you might remember to thank your family and friends, but thank *everyone* who claps for you when you walk onto the stage to claim your trophy. You may not know them, but their applause signifies their support, and that's helping you reach your goals.

CHAPTER 48

S ummer ended with me still riding high because of the NWSL championship. But soon it was time to return to the national team.

In the fall and winter of 2013, my teammates and I were training for a series of friendly games, and we were feeling great about being back together with our new coach. We'd had one game in September, and before that we hadn't played since June. But in October we had three games scheduled in quick succession: one against Australia and two against New Zealand. We'd beaten Australia 4–0 and were looking forward to doing the same against New Zealand.

But on a closed-door scrimmage against Australia—an unofficial, unpublicized game—something happened to my left ankle. Abby and I had entered the match in the seventieth minute when we were down 2–1. We had made a pact while warming up that we would get that goal back. So we went in, and with time draining in the match, I took on a defender and lost the ball. I tracked the defender down and went in to tackle her, but when I went for the ball, I sprained my ankle—badly. I immediately knew something was very wrong, and soon my ankle swelled up larger than a softball.

"Well, we'll do an MRI just to make sure everything's okay, but I'm fairly confident it's just a sprain," said the team doctor. *Whew.* I'd had ankle sprains before. It's a three-week injury. No big deal.

I knew I wouldn't be playing against New Zealand in the next game, but maybe I'd be back for the following game.

Sure enough, the MRI confirmed what the doctor had said. It was just a sprain. Rest up, do a little physical therapy, and I'd be back in no time.

I sat on the sidelines and watched us beat New Zealand in our next two games, and pretty soon I was back on the field practicing. I still didn't feel 100 percent, but I attributed that to having been out for a little bit. I was just rusty.

And just like that, I was playing again on November 11 in a friendly game against Brazil. Tom was pretty cautious and decided to put me in as a second-half sub, but I promised myself I'd be patient. *Don't be impatient, Alex,* I told myself. *He's looking out for you, and a little rest never hurt anyone.* So I took it easy, then went into the game in the sixty-eighth minute and helped our team beat Brazil 4–1.

Believe it or not, we were already starting to think about the World Cup qualifying tournament, which was going to be held the following fall. I couldn't believe it had been almost four years since I burst onto the international scene—I felt like I'd known my teammates all my life. We'd gone through so many highs and lows—a devastating World Cup defeat, an exhilarating Olympic win, the loss of our coach, the gaining of a new one. Abby and Tobin and Sydney and everyone else were my family, and we were all counting the days till we could go to the World Cup again. Nothing was going to stop me, least of all an ankle sprain.

But as I continued training, something just didn't feel right. My recovery had plateaued at about 80 percent. The doctors were telling me that I was fine, but I knew I wasn't. You should always trust yourself—nobody knows your body better than you. I wasn't getting better, and that wasn't like me. My injuries had always healed with the proper treatment, but I kept feeling pain. What was going on?

Feelings of dread were coming over me, but I pushed them away. When things aren't going well, you just can't imagine the worst—it's not going to help. I told myself to think positive and continue talking to my doctors, and I decided to get another MRI.

"Well, the news isn't as good as we hoped," my

orthopedist said with a look of concern on his face. "You've gone backward instead of forward. It looks like playing on your sprained ankle caused a bone bruise, and you've got a stress reaction. You're going to need to be on crutches for a few weeks."

I knew what a stress reaction was. It's the first stage of a bone injury, and if it accelerates, the bone will fracture. Essentially, when you have a stress fracture, you're repeatedly injuring your bone faster than it can rebuild itself. The only cure is to put no stress on the bone, allowing it to heal.

Crutches? I was in disbelief. And I was so, so angry. The doctors and trainers had thought I could play, yet working out had made it worse. How could this happen to me? I had to keep training. I'd be going back to the Thorns soon, and the US team would be training for the Algarve Cup, and then there was the World Cup qualifying tournament. A few weeks of lost training could put me back months. So much was at stake.

In utter despair, I went back home. Nothing seemed right in my world anymore, and nothing was going to fix it at that moment.

Trust Your Gut

I knew my injury was worse than the doctors thought, so I pushed hard to get a new diagnosis. I know my body, and believing in that helped me finally find the reason for my injury. Trust your gut—you know what's best for you. If you feel something's wrong, don't be afraid to speak up. You might be wrong, but at least you'll know. If you don't act on your instincts, though, you might never get the answer you're looking for.

CHAPTER 49

There are few benefits to having your dreams pushed aside. It's incredibly hard having to change directions and pursue other goals, but I promise you, if you just open your heart and let people in when things are bad, they just might make you feel better.

My teammates couldn't have been nicer to me. I got texts and calls and e-mails all the time, and people stopped by just to see how I was doing. My parents called me almost every day, and my dad constantly reminded me that I'd had it worse when I injured my ACL—I'd had to go in for surgery back then! And look what I'd done since—I'd only gotten better. Abby had broken her leg a few years back (right before the Olympics!) and she was a stronger player than she'd ever been. This could make *me* stronger, and I just had to tell myself that again and again.

And then there was my boyfriend. With nonstop training and different schedules, Servando and I hadn't had any downtime in the last few years. He was now playing for the Houston Dynamo, and it had been hard not to see him as often in person.

But with me off the field, I could spend more time with Servando. I moved to Houston, and it was great for our relationship. In all our time together, we'd always had totally different schedules. Now it was nice to spend so much time in each other's presence, not having a long-distance relationship. Plus, it was great not living out of a suitcase!

So even though I was miserable being on crutches, I had happiness in my life—a lot of it. That's the funny thing about being down and out: It makes the bright, happy moments feel even better. It's like when there are clouds filling the sky and the sun pokes its way through—it's almost prettier than a sunny day.

On a beautiful night that December, Servando and I got engaged. We had been talking about getting married for a while, but it was still a perfect surprise—one that I got to celebrate with family and friends. It also happened at a time I needed it most. I'd felt vulnerable and at times miserable, but I was growing as a person despite it all. When you're feeling low, just know that glimmers of happiness are out there somewhere. People may be kind to you when you're feeling your worst, and something unexpectedly wonderful may happen, bringing a smile to your face.

Be Optimistic

See? Sometimes when things are at their worst, great things can happen. Happiness often shows up when you least expect it. Even though rehab and being on crutches was difficult in so many ways, I got to spend valuable time with my boyfriend and start to plan a life together with him. We grew stronger despite what I was going through. So always be optimistic—good things might be just around the corner!

CHAPTER 50

A s 2014 began, I still wasn't physically where I needed to be. I'd gone through several doctors and had more MRIs, but the source of the problem was still a mystery. I was on crutches for three weeks, and when I went to see my doctor, I expected her to tell me I could stop using them. She rescanned my foot, said there had been little improvement, and told me to stay on crutches for three *more* weeks. I didn't think I'd be able to take it. *Six full weeks on crutches?* I thought.

After those additional three weeks, the doctors finally discovered that I had a partially torn ligament in my ankle, which meant I was going to have to wear a protective boot for several weeks. Thankfully, I wouldn't have to have surgery, but I was going to have to stay put and let myself heal some more.

The US national team was going to a training camp from January 8–15, then playing Canada on the thirty-first, and I wasn't going to be there. My heart was broken, and things were starting to seem more and more hope-less. I hadn't been off the field this long since my ACL injury in high school, and so much less was at stake then.

What was hardest was that it was difficult to set goals while I was injured. As you know, I've been setting goals since I was a kid—get a scholarship, get to the World Cup, win the Olympics—but now all of my dreams were dependent on getting better. Then I realized that *was* my goal. I had to do everything possible to heal myself.

Sometimes, in order to get where you want to go, you have to turn inward. Your goals are probably all about reaching certain milestones, but oftentimes, your goals need to be much more personal. They may entail one thing: taking care of yourself. If you can do that, then you can conquer the bigger obstacles in front of you.

Taking care of myself paid off. Sometime that winter, I started to see the light at the end of the tunnel. The final diagnosis seemed to be the right one, and stabilizing my foot in the boot had actually started to heal it. My coaches on the US team and on the Thorns were patient, which meant the world to me. They believed that I'd be back where I'd been three months before, which helped me believe it too.

In late February Tom Sermanni announced the roster for the Algarve Cup, and I wasn't on it, but I wasn't sur-prised. I was in consideration, but given that I'd hardly trained with the team and was still touch and go, Tom didn't want to risk reinjuring my ankle. That had been the whole problem to begin with.

In the meantime, I decided to set realistic goals for myself. I knew I had to be conservative in order to prevent further injury. I couldn't take fifty extra shots after practice, for example. I'd be patient and work hard, but work *smart*. My goals were simple: try to make every shot as good as possible so I could take fewer and build up my speed slowly. Going too fast too soon wasn't going to help me at all. If I could master these two fundamentals, I knew I'd be playing again soon.

Don't Set Only Big Goals

When you're sidelined, in sports or in life, setting smaller, realistic goals for yourself is probably the best thing you can do. You might have felt the sky was the limit before your dreams took a wrong turn, but that doesn't mean that accomplishing small tasks can't be satisfying. Just remember that as you accomplish small things, you're on your way to doing bigger things in the future. No goal is too small—it's accomplishing them that counts.

CHAPTER 51

Being away from the national team was hard. I hadn't missed a tournament with them in three years, and not being at the Algarve Cup—especially after our big win again Germany last year—didn't feel right. It was so cool to see new players on the Algarve Cup roster, though. Morgan Brian, Samantha Mewis, and Sarah Killion were all still in college, and in fact, Morgan was turning twenty-one the day she arrived in Portugal! I felt like a veteran compared to them, but of course, I had been in their shoes so recently. Having new faces on the team—combined with fifteen older players who'd been to Portugal before—was a good omen for us. We'd always thrived on a mixture of experience and energy.

But it didn't work for us. In fact, it didn't work *at all*. I checked in from home regularly and was so disappointed to see us finish last in the group stage with one tie and two losses. That meant we didn't advance to the finals, and we had to settle for a seventh-place match against North Korea. Thankfully, we won 3–0. It was Heather O'Reilly's two hundredth appearance in an international game. On the one hand, it was a celebration for Heather, but on the other, no one expected us to get seventh place. We were the best in the world—Olympic champions and the winners of last year's Cup!

I couldn't stop feeling terrible about the whole thing. *If I'd been there, would it have been different? Would we have advanced to the finals, like we always had?* I had to push those feelings aside. A team is not about one person—or it shouldn't be. The US national team was most certainly not. We had Tobin and Abby and Megan and Hope and every other player who'd made us the strongest team in the world. It wasn't about one person who scored a lot of goals. We were great because we had excellent goalkeepers, strikers, midfielders, and defenders and because we played our hearts out *together*. Wins were group efforts, and unfortunately, so were losses. And I was feeling it even though I wasn't on the field.

The press was throwing around the word "disaster" when they referenced our seventh-place finish, and I know we felt like that at times. But we just had to keep moving forward. This was a misstep, but it wasn't something we couldn't fix. We had the World Cup qualifying tournament in the fall, and I knew we could dominate it. It was all about confidence, hard work, and teamwork. We'd mastered those things before, and we could do it again.

• • •

You always have to remember that there are things in life that are out of your control. Decisions are often made that you can't do anything about, so while you may have strong objections—or quite the opposite, think it's the greatest thing in the world—there's nothing you can do. You just have to let go.

That's what the US team had to do when our head coach was fired in early April. You heard it right—Tom Sermanni was released from his contract with the national team after less than a year and a half. Just a few weeks after the Algarve Cup and hours after we'd won a friendly game against China while I was still sidelined, Tom got the news. And the next day, we received it too. He was gone, just like that.

The announcement from US Soccer was succinct. "We felt that we needed to go in a different direction at this time." Tom admitted publicly he was shocked, and to be honest, so were we—coaches just aren't fired that suddenly. But we weren't surprised because there had been some issues. Many of the experienced players felt they hadn't been pushed enough, and they thought the coaching staff's expectations of them had noticeably dropped. It was as if Tom thought there was enough talent on the team that we didn't have to keep fighting. Being too relaxed and not nurturing that ultra-competitive, hard-driven culture had caused us to drop games and perform badly in the Algarve Cup, and that's when US Soccer decided they had to do something. It was now or never: If they didn't fire him then, it would be too late to salvage our chances for the World Cup.

Tom spoke to the team after he was fired, and I had so much respect for that. He could have just walked away, but he felt he owed us something, so he gave us one last pep talk and said good-bye. Abby spoke for all of us when she said, "I wish he was a jerk in some ways because it would be easier. But that's just not the case. He's such a good guy. He treated us all with the utmost respect and we wish him nothing but the best of luck."

We couldn't dwell on the firing, though—there just wasn't time. We had to look ahead to the 2015 World Cup, and we had had to start training hard.

Face Sudden Change with Courage

Sudden change is hard, but it's part of life. When it happens, don't think it's the end of the world. Just focus on your goals and stay strong. If you have people you can talk to who are going through the same thing you are, do so. Talking to my teammates was so helpful after Tom was fired. I had been away recovering from my injury when it happened, so speaking with them helped me understand what had transpired. Have courage—you *can* make it through whatever life throws your way.

CHAPTER 52

I had been dreaming of my first goal after getting back on the field. Literally having dreams about it. I wanted to play so badly, and by the beginning of summer, I thought it might be possible: My ankle was doing *much* better.

I'd been practicing and scrimmaging pretty regularly with the Thorns, but never straining myself too hard. Then one day during practice, Rachel Buehler tackled me. I went down, and amazingly, I didn't even think of my ankle. I didn't feel a thing, and no fear crossed my mind.

And then I realized: I was ready to play full-time.

I had one final MRI just to be sure, and what's so funny is that I read the report myself! I'd had so many MRIs that I felt like an amateur radiologist. I knew my ankle backward and forward and checked every bit of the scan just to be sure it looked right. And it did.

On June 7, I returned to the field in a game against Western New York. I was *so* happy. I hadn't played in seven months—the longest stretch I'd ever been away from soccer—and being back on the field was going to be a celebration for me. We lost to Western New York 5–0, which didn't make any of us happy, but just being there reminded me of how much I'd missed playing.

Just a week later I got to play with the national team too. Jill Ellis was serving as our interim coach, and things were going well with her. She was a familiar face—she'd been an assistant coach under Pia, then the interim coach after Pia's departure in 2012—so having her with us felt like a smooth transition. And being back on the field was natural for me too. I was subbed in during the forty-sixth minute and helped our team win 1–0 against France. It was so much fun being back!

There's always so much pressure when you return after a long hiatus. And it's mostly internal. When you're a forward, you have extra tension because everyone expects you to score, but I actually like that. It motivates me, so I embrace it. If you feel pressure to perform, especially after being away from something for a while, don't let it intimidate you. Just view the stress as something that can help you forge ahead.

Unfortunately, I got a big scare in mid-July in a game against Kansas City. Everything was going well, and then I was hit on the inside of my right ankle. That was my good ankle! I went down and noticed immediately that everything was numb. No pain, just numbness. A stretcher was brought onto the field, and the trainers carried me off.

Thankfully, it was nothing serious. I'd just hit a nerve, and soon the feeling came back. But it was a wake-up call. I'd been so excited to be back, and suddenly I was faced with the prospect of being injured again! It just goes to show you can never take anything for granted, especially your health.

The season was as rocky for the Portland Thorns as my health had been. Our hearts were in it, but we just weren't as strong as we'd been in 2013. We lost games we should have won (like the 5–0 loss to Western New York Flash) and didn't come together in ways I wish we had. Still, the fans showed up: We broke our attendance record when more than nineteen thousand people watched us in a game against Houston.

We did not finish on top that season. We made it to the semifinals after a thrilling win against Seattle—Allie Long had made a corner kick in the sixty-eighth minute, and I headed it into the goal right past Hope Solo—but then we lost to Kansas City in the semis. Of course, we were disappointed, but we had played hard. And there was always next year.

For my part, I was just happy to be playing again.

Don't Take Anything for Granted

If the first half of 2014 had taught me anything, it was never to take things for granted. Life can change at a moment's notice. My right ankle injury was terrifying, and I'm so lucky it wasn't worse. And the failure of the Thorns to make it past the semifinals was hard—after all, we'd won so decisively the year before. Always be thankful for successes, good health, and everything else you're blessed with in your life, and never assume that you'll just always have them.

CHAPTER 53

The CONCACAF World Cup qualifying tournament was the first thing on everyone's minds at the end of the summer. We were so ready and so confident. Jill Ellis had officially been named head coach, and we felt like we'd found some stability with her. She was a modern coach, utilizing video analysis and statistics in a way that Tom hadn't. She also strongly believed in communication, frequently meeting with us one-on-one to let us know where we stood. And she'd been around the team so much before she was named head coach so she knew our culture. It was a great fit, and our play would prove it.

We won all our friendly games at the end of the summer, and as we headed into the fall, Jill named the CONCACAF qualifying tournament roster. There were twenty of us on the list, and eleven of us had been to the World Cup before. That meant there were a lot of newcomers! But I loved this team. There was depth in every position, the play at the training camps had been excellent, and all in all, we were mentally and physically strong.

This was going to be an interesting tournament. First off, Canada wouldn't be playing since they were guaranteed entry into the World Cup as the host country. And second, we'd be playing on US soil—four stadiums across the United States—so we'd be in front of our own fans. We were always better when the twelfth player was on our side, so this would be great for us.

Our first game was against Trinidad and Tobago. They were playing under an American coach who was doing it strictly on a volunteer basis, and they had been sent to the United States with only five hundred dollars given by their national soccer federation. They spent three hundred dollars on meals during a stopover in Miami, and then the remaining two hundred dollars to get from the airport in Dallas to their hotel. By the time they arrived there, they had no money to actually *pay* for the hotel, no equipment, and nothing to eat. They had to solicit donations from the local and international community just to get lunch. Thankfully, their coach's tweets helped them raise enough to cover everything during their stay, and the Dallas Trinidadian community hosted several dinners for them.

Trinidad and Tobago played better than anyone expected, but for us, the game was nerve-racking, all too close, and we felt nothing had gone our way. Thankfully, we pulled it off in the second half. I crossed the ball to Abby in the fifty-fourth minute, and in her signature move, she headed it right in. We just squeaked a win out with a final score of 1–0. It wasn't our best start to the tournament.

Despite that, I loved being back with the national team, and one of the best parts was being reunited with Abby. We hadn't played together for much of 2014, and we'd really missed each other. We always thought about each other when we plotted out our strategy on the field, and we consistently made better plays together.

We headed into our October 17 game against Guatemala feeling great. If we won this match, we'd be guaranteed entry into the CONCACAF semifinals. Guatemala was coming off a disappointing loss to Haiti, so we predicted it wouldn't be a tough game. We were hopeful, positive, and full of steam.

And I was feeling strong. My ankle was stable, and my performances on the field had been terrific. I was looking ahead and thinking positive.

But unfortunately, it's times like that when life decides to test you again. . . .

We'd all woken up that Friday morning so excited. Like I said, if we beat Guatemala, we'd be going to the semifinals. We were playing outside of Chicago, in front of an enthusiastic crowd, and we knew we were poised for victory. Sydney and I were set to start as forwards, with Abby on the bench for a possible late-game substitution.

This time we were dominant from the moment the whistle blew. Tobin shot from inside the goal box in the seventh minute and scored decisively. And for much of the rest of the first half, we took over the field.

In the thirty-seventh minute, the Guatemalan goalkeeper punted the ball into a crowd of players. We secured it, and then a midfielder passed the ball to me as I sprinted toward the goal. While gaining control, I was flanked by two defenders who were doing a pretty good job of slowing me down, but I kept going. I began leaning toward the right, as if to shield my body between the ball and the defender. At that moment, I stepped wrong, and my ankle turned in ninety degrees. I felt an excruciating pain shoot through it.

It was my left ankle. The one I'd spent seven months rehabbing. The ankle I hadn't put any weight on for six weeks while I hobbled around on crutches. That same ankle had me on the ground, writhing in pain.

I was terrified. *What had I done? Could this really be happening again?* I couldn't afford to be out for the next seven months. I couldn't afford to be out for three months! I was getting married later that year, and what was I going to do—walk down the aisle on crutches?

But more immediately, I wanted to play with my team throughout this tournament and see us advance to the World Cup. I'd spent months and years working for this, and one bad slip had jeopardized that.

Of course, I hadn't seen myself fall, but if you watch it on YouTube, it looks terrible. My ankle twists inward in a pretty gruesome fashion, and watching it, I'm surprised I didn't break it. When the stretcher took me off the field, I was so upset I felt myself struggling to breathe. *How can this be happening again?*

Of course, the doctors tended to me immediately, and the first few things they said were a big relief.

"It's not broken."

Well, at least there was that, and that was huge.

"I think it's just a sprain. But we'll find out tomorrow when you get an MRI."

I was hoping against hope that it wasn't a torn ligament or worse, and when the MRI came back the next day, it was good news. It was a sprain. There was absolutely no evidence of any other damage.

Still, I was going to be out for four to six weeks, which meant missing the rest of the CONCACAF tournament. We had beaten Guatemala decisively the night before, 5–0, so we were advancing to the semifinals against Mexico—the team who had given us so much trouble in the last CONCACAF tournament. I longed to be there, but I came to peace with the fact that I wouldn't and that my team would be fine without me.

Give Yourself a Break

I've talked a lot about how you should never stop working in order to reach your goals. But that doesn't mean you have to work twenty-four hours a day, seven days a week *forever*. When you've reached a level of success, you can give yourself a break. I don't mean you should slack off and let things fall apart in your absence, but if your presence isn't needed for a period of time, let yourself rest. I knew my team would be okay without me— we had other forwards who were just as capable as I was and could fill my shoes while I was away. Sure enough, I didn't stress out while I was sidelined, and things were just fine.

CHAPTER 54

During my previous rehab—the one that lasted seven agonizing months—I had been too hasty. I'd been so frustrated by my lack of a good diagnosis and the mixed signals I was getting— *You're going off crutches! You're going back on crutches!*— that I'd probably tested my limits a little too much. In the beginning that had meant my sprain turned into a stress reaction, but at the end it just meant that I was getting frustrated by feeling "behind."

There is no "behind" when you're setting goals. You are where you are. Feeling defeated just because you haven't reached a milestone by an arbitrary date is silly, or at worst, destructive. Take your time and go easy on yourself. No one, least of all yourself, should rush you.

That's what I told myself as I sat on my couch and watched the national team progress in the CONCACAF World Cup qualifying tournament. I was going to be cautious and conservative. I was going to take it easy and set a realistic goal for myself, which was to go to

Brazil for the International Tournament of Brasilia in December. I wouldn't push myself or kick myself for not being at the qualifying tournament. Instead, I was just going to chill.

And besides, I had a wedding to plan and a bachelorette party to attend!

Servando and I were getting married in the winter, and I was so excited. I'd been preparing and planning for months, but it was all starting to become real. To me, a wedding isn't just about the party or the dress. It's about family and friends. I've been a bridesmaid a few times and have gone to many weddings, and seeing people in love, surrounded by all the people in their lives, is inspiring. That's what I wanted for my wedding.

But first I wanted to see the national team advance in the World Cup qualifying tournament. And as I rested, rehabbed, and dreamed of being a bride back in Houston, much to my delight, they did!

The United States beat Haiti decisively in the last game in the group stage, then went on to the semifinals against Mexico. Remember what happened against Mexico in the last CONCACAF tournament? That was *not* going to happen again.

We were the favorites to win, but it was still a thrilling victory. Carli Lloyd scored two goals in the first half, then Christen Press scored in the second half, giving the United States a 3–0 victory.

But what was even more exciting was seeing our cocaptain, Christie Rampone, celebrate her three hundredth international game. At thirty-nine years old, she was behind only Kristine Lilly in terms of the number of international appearances. I was so happy for her, and my respect for her made my heart swell. She'd bounced back to soccer after having two kids and battling Lyme disease, which can be almost crippling. She is an example of strength, determination, and beautiful leadership, and I am honored to call her my teammate.

The final game of the World Cup qualifying tournament was set for October 26 against Costa Rica. With an appearance in the final, we were guaranteed to go to the World Cup, so while the end result didn't matter, winning would be so sweet.

We won 6–0 in a victory that was beautiful to watch. Abby scored a first-half hat trick, broke the World Cup qualifying goal record, and made a total of four goals in the game. Hope hadn't let a single ball get by her the whole tournament, which made our goal record for the tournament 21–0. If anyone had doubted us, this really showed we were the best in the world.

It was hard not being there, but my happiness for the

team overrode any sadness I was feeling. And besides, I was getting better, which made me more confident by the day. My goal was to go to Brazil, and I knew I would get there. Then it was on to the World Cup. . . .

Find Inspiration in Others

Christie Rampone is thirty-nine years old and shows no sign of slowing down. She's played in four World Cups and has won Olympic gold three times. She's participated in more international games than any active soccer player in the world, and she's second on the all-time list. She's come back to soccer after having two kids and after fighting a devastating battle against Lyme disease, which left her so exhausted that she struggled to play. Christie is an inspiration to me, and I look to her as an example of strength, confidence, and leadership. Christie is more than just a mentor—she's someone I can look to when I think, *I need motivation*. Find someone who provides this for you—you don't have to know them, but just having them in the back of your mind will drive you as you work toward your goals.

CHAPTER 55

Life is about so much more than the pursuit of your goals. I'm not downplaying going after your dreams, of course, but what I'm saying is that you should never stop thinking about the world around you.

Soccer hasn't been my only dream in life, and resting and rehabbing helped me think about what else is important to me. It's made me want to help others even more. I'm a public person now—I have a fan base and people who want my thoughts about issues—and I want to give back now more than ever.

I've been active in a lot of charities over the years. In 2011, Abby Wambach, Hope Solo, and I ran the Chicago Marathon on behalf of the American Society for the Prevention of Cruelty of Animals, or the ASPCA. I *love* animals and have a little cat named Brooklyn whom I adore, so animal rights are very important to me.

I also work to support the Susan G. Komen Breast Cancer Foundation. I didn't know Servando's mom when she was first diagnosed with breast cancer, but I've watched her struggle with the fear that it may come back. Thankfully, she was given a clean bill of health five years after her initial diagnosis and continues to have cancer-free checkups. But breast cancer affects more women than any other kind of cancer, and raising money and awareness is key to finding a cure.

I work a lot with kids, too. Aside from doing soccer clinics and talking about injury prevention, I love to speak with girls about goal setting, teamwork, and having good role models. That was so important to me as a girl, and I'd love other girls to feel as inspired as I felt when I first began following women's soccer. I've done inner-city soccer programs, spoken to thousands of young women (and men!) around the country, and attended elementary and high schools.

I was thrust into the spotlight when I was in my early twenties, which is pretty early. There's a lot of pressure associated with that. I know how much I looked up to Kristine Lilly and Mia Hamm when I was a kid, so I strive to be that kind of role model to girls now. What I say on Twitter, the photos I show on Instagram, and my quotes in the press influence others, so I always try to be upbeat and inspirational. I want young people to feel positive about themselves and life, so I try to be the same. I also want my fans to embrace their identities. If you're a chess club star, own it! If you're a strong, athletic woman like me, don't be afraid to show it. I never want people to try to change who they are.

I write a book series called The Kicks about a group of middle-school-aged girls who play on a California soccer team. The books focus on teamwork, having good role models, and overcoming obstacles, and they're inspirational and fun at the same time. I have so much fun writing these books, and I love hearing from fans about them. Each book draws on my own experiences playing soccer growing up, and my hope has been that each teaches something. Through the stories and the characters, my goal has been to empower young girls.

Don't ever let anyone tell you that because you're young you don't matter or that your opinion and ideas don't count. You *are* the future. That's why learning how to set goals now is so important—it's a tool you'll need for the rest of your life. You'll modify them, scrap some of them, and build upon others, but your goals will help you grow into the person you want to be. When I work with young people, I want them to know that they are important, and I want them to strive to be better people. If I can give back something to them, maybe they'll give back too.

Charity can be big or small, but make it a part of your life. Even if you have no money to give, as I've said before, give your time. And be an example to others. When your light shines brightly, it illuminates the world around you.

Remember That You Matter

You might go to a huge high school and feel like a number rather than a person, or you might not have any close friends, making you feel like an outcast. But you matter. Your ideas, goals, and feelings are important, and don't let anyone tell you otherwise. If you feel lonely now, things will change, I promise. Middle school and high school can be very tough, but it will get easier. Just continue to find inspiration in the things you love, and never give up hope. I promise that everyone has felt all alone, but it doesn't last forever.

CHAPTER 56

I rested, I did physical therapy, and sure enough, my left ankle healed just like I knew it would. And when the roster for December's International Tournament of Brasilia was announced, I was on it along with twenty-three of my teammates. I'd made my post-injury goal!

No one on the team had played in Brazil except for Christie Rampone, who'd played there in 1997. Jill spoke for all of us when she said, "It's a chance to travel to a new environment and play international matches in unfamiliar territory, which is always valuable when getting ready for a World Cup. It's a unique opportunity to go to a fantastic soccer country, have a great cultural experience, and play four competitive games to end the year on a high note."

We'd be playing in a World Cup stadium—the second-most-expensive stadium in the world, after Wembley in London—and it was spectacular. We'd play one of our four games against our old foe China, one against Argentina, another against Brazil, and the last against a team to be determined. We hadn't played Argentina since 1998.

We knew tournament play would be challenging and fun, but in many ways, this was a warm-up for the World Cup, which was already causing us to be on pins and needles. The World Cup draw, which determined the game schedule, was going to be on December 5, the day before I was flying to Brazil. During the draw, the names of the top-seeded teams are placed in one pot, with the rest of the competing nations divided into three other pots on the basis of their continental governing body.

Have you ever watched the lottery, where someone pulls balls out of a spinning globe? That's sort of what happens in the World Cup draw. Four officials pull out balls at random, which determines the placement of the six groups for the group stage of the World Cup. It's a real show—there's dancing and a mascot and lots of lights. It's over-the-top, but a lot of fun.

We drew an incredibly challenging group. So tough that it was immediately dubbed the Group of Death. Group D contained us, Sweden (Pia's team!), Australia (the #10 team in the world), and Nigeria (always the best team in Africa). On June 6, we'd be heading into action, and we knew every day and every game till then were going to be warm-ups for what lay ahead.

I landed in Brazil with my thoughts centered on the World Cup draw. If anything, the fact that our opponents would be so tough was motivating. As I've said before, I thrive on pressure, and there's nothing I like more than good competition.

The overall reaction of the team was happiness. Our midfielder Lauren Cheney said, "We were laughing in a good way" and added, "It is a 'bring-it-on' attitude, one hundred percent. Everyone says that we got the hardest group draw, and it probably is. But for us that's just another obstacle, and we love pressure. We're very excited and we're ready to play."

So as we headed into Brazil, we were thinking about June, ready to play our hardest and completely fired up. Soccer is a joy, especially when you love your teammates, and nothing could be closer to the truth for me. My team is my family, and we're all in this together, ready to do whatever we can to reach our goals.

And right now we all have the same goal: win the 2015 World Cup.

Enjoy Challenges

Embrace the pressure in your life. It's there to motivate you, not to bring you down! Of course, if you're feeling so stressed that it's interfering with your work, you need to stop, breathe, and refocus. But a challenge shouldn't be considered an obstacle—if anything, it's a fun hill to climb! It will get your heart pumping and make you stronger. That's how we're viewing "the Group of Death" right now. We're so fired up that we can't wait to play!

CHAPTER 57

I f you believe in something deep down in your heart, you have to speak up. Your opinion matters, and it may help enact change. When something in the world just isn't right, it takes a motivated group of people to protest it, and that's where you come in. Don't just stand by and let things roll over you—you *can* make a difference.

The 2015 World Cup is going to be played entirely on artificial turf. I'm among forty-plus international players who have filed a lawsuit against FIFA, protesting this decision based on gender discrimination. The men's World Cup is played on grass, a surface that is far friendlier to your body.

I've been hurt so many times, and I know that serious injuries happen more often when you're playing on turf. Your cleats get stuck in the ground more easily, which can cause falls. Turf's harder than grass, so this can lead to torn ligaments, broken bones, layers of skin peeling off your arms and legs, and concussions. Abby refuses to do diving headers on turf, so it diminishes the quality of her play. I'm much sorer after I play on turf, and it takes longer to recover. With an extra round in this year's Cup, recovery is crucial—and you just don't have that after a turf game.

It was 159 degrees on the turf one day during a game I played in the summer, and I was so horrified I took a photo of a thermometer on the turf and tweeted it. It can get hot up in Canada, too, so we're at risk of actually being burned while playing. How is that healthy?

But worst of all, some think that playing on turf may lead to cancer. You remember my freshman-year roommate, Jorden LaFontaine-Kussmann, who developed lymphoma? She believes her cancer was linked to playing on artificial turf. Turf is made up of small particles that are actually chunks of tires. When you fall on turf, thousands of these particles go into the air, so you're breathing tires into your lungs. If you have a cut, the chemicals in the tires go right into your bloodstream, or if you scrape yourself, the turf particles stick to your skin, and your skin grows over them. A University of Washington coach named Amy Griffin has compiled a list of thirty-eight soccer players in the United States—thirty-four of them goalkeepers—who have contracted cancer, most of them blood-based cancers like leukemia and lymphoma. If you think of how many times a goalkeeper falls to the ground—dozens of times a day—you can imagine what kind of exposure to toxic chemicals they're experiencing.

While there hasn't been a comprehensive study that links turf to cancer, I think it's only a matter of time. The issue is very new, but there's been a lot of press coverage about it, so I feel sure the research will back us. I just hope no one dies from cancer before that.

The men's World Cup didn't allow turf, and they built multimillion dollar stadiums (totaling more than three billion dollars) specifically for the tournament, with all-grass fields. If the men can have that, why not us? The fight isn't over, and I'll keep battling to get awareness out about this issue. I've tweeted about it, spoken to the press, and thrown my name into a lawsuit that speaks volumes about the fight for gender equality in sports. This isn't just about turf. It's about female athletes receiving the same treatment as male athletes. I believe FIFA has long favored men's soccer over women's, and they need to change their outlook. They need to accept women as footballers too—we shouldn't be given any less attention. We've worked just as hard as the men to get to where we are, and we want to be treated as equals.

Speak Up

Don't be afraid to speak up. The most influential people in the world—from Martin Luther King Jr. to Gandhi to

Susan B. Anthony—fought against popular opinion to make change in the world. If they hadn't stood up for what they believed was right, they would have never conquered their goals of making the world a better place. You can do the same in big and small ways. If you think your school isn't taking its recycling program seriously enough, start a petition. If you believe someone's being bullied in your school, defend them and talk to a guidance counselor. Be strong and bold and fight for what's right!

Afterword

I struggled a lot with the right way to end this book. I never expected to be writing something about my life when I'm only twenty-five and so much is just beginning. So an ending? It feels odd. There's really no wrap-up to my story, and in many ways, I'll always be writing it!

The same is true for you. Your life will constantly be evolving and changing, and every day will likely be different. Each time the sun comes up you have a new opportunity to work toward making your dreams come true, and even when you say good-bye to something (like a friend who's moving or a school year), you're going to begin something else (you'll meet a new friend or start a new year).

I don't profess to be an authority on much except for soccer, but I do know that hard work pays off, teamwork can make anything easier, and thinking positively will make you happier. I've learned most of this on the soccer field, but you may learn it at school, over the dinner

table, while taking a test, or on a long hike up a mountain. Whatever you do, I hope you enjoy every second of
the work that goes into making your dreams come true.
Achieving a goal is a beautiful thing, but it won't happen
unless you stop and plot out what your dreams are, then
work like crazy to make them come true. And believe
me, you can do it!

Servando and I celebrated our wedding on December
31, 2014. Getting married on New Year's felt so right for
us—much like one year ending and another beginning,
we were closing out a chapter of our lives and starting a
new one. As I said to the press, "I truly married my best
friend," and I was so lucky I got to do it in front of my
teammates, my family, and friends I'd known since I was
a little girl. As people counted down the seconds till the
clock struck midnight, I don't remember much except
feeling happy, loved, and supremely grateful. I've had
such a blessed life.

But I've worked for it, and I've had ups and downs
and setbacks that, at times, I thought were permanent.
What's pushed me through all the rough patches in my
personal and professional lives was the belief that something better is always in front of me. Never, ever stop
thinking this—you can work to make your life fuller and
richer each day.

By the time you read this, the 2015 World Cup may

be under way, or it may be long over. I can guarantee you one thing: No matter where we are, my teammates and I are living out our dreams on the soccer field. We love what we're doing in part because we believe in one another, we practice with our goals in mind, and we know we can always keep improving.

I hope you embrace the opportunity to do the same.

Dream big. Love life. And never stop pursuing your goals.

—Alex Morgan, January 2015

Pine River Library
395 Bayfield Center Dr.
P.O. Box 227
Bayfield, CO 81122
(970) 884-2222
www.prlibrary.org